HEALTH CARE ISSUES, COSTS AND ACCESS

HEALTH INSURANCE EXCHANGES UNDER THE AFFORDABLE CARE ACT

HEALTH CARE ISSUES, COSTS AND ACCESS

Additional books in this series can be found on Nova's website under the Series tab.

Additional E-books in this series can be found on Nova's website under the E-book tab.

HEALTH CARE IN TRANSITION

Additional books in this series can be found on Nova's website under the Series tab.

Additional E-books in this series can be found on Nova's website under the E-book tab.

HEALTH CARE ISSUES, COSTS AND ACCESS

HEALTH INSURANCE EXCHANGES UNDER THE AFFORDABLE CARE ACT

EDWARD J. VOLPICELLI
EDITOR

NOVINKA

New York

For permission to use material from this book please contact us:
Telephone 631-231-7269; Fax 631-231-8175
Web Site: http://www.novapublishers.com

Additional color graphics may be available in the e-book version of this book.

Library of Congress Cataloging-in-Publication Data

ISBN: 978-1-62417-367-7

Published by Nova Science Publishers, Inc. † New York

CONTENTS

PREFACE

The fundamental purpose of a health insurance exchange is to provide a structured marketplace for the sale and purchase of health insurance. The authority and responsibilities of an exchange may vary, depending on statutory or other requirements for its establishment and structure. The Patient Protection and Affordable Care Act (ACA) requires health insurance exchanges to be established in every state by January 1, 2014. ACA provides certain requirements for the establishment of exchanges, while leaving other choices to be made by the states. This book outlines the required minimum functions of exchanges, and explains how exchanges are expected to be established and administered under ACA. The coverage offered through exchanges is discussed, as are how the exchanges will interact with selected other ACA provisions.

Chapter 1 – The fundamental purpose of a health insurance exchange is to provide a structured marketplace for the sale and purchase of health insurance. The authority and responsibilities of an exchange may vary, depending on statutory or other requirements for its establishment and structure.

The Patient Protection and Affordable Care Act (ACA, P.L. 111-148, as amended) requires health insurance exchanges to be established in every state by January 1, 2014. ACA provides certain requirements for the establishment of exchanges, while leaving other choices to be made by the states.

Qualified individuals and small businesses will be able to purchase private health insurance through exchanges. Issuers selling health insurance plans through an exchange will have to follow certain rules, such as meeting the private market reform requirements in ACA. While the fundamental purpose of the exchanges will be to facilitate the offer and purchase of health insurance, nothing in the law prohibits qualified individuals, qualified employers, and insurance carriers from participating in the health insurance market outside of exchanges. Moreover, ACA explicitly states that enrollment in exchanges is voluntary and no individual may be compelled to enroll in exchange coverage.

Chapter 2 – New federal tax credits were authorized in the Patient Protection and Affordable Care Act (ACA, P.L. 111-148, as amended), to help certain individuals pay for health insurance coverage, beginning in 2014.

ACA requires "American Health Benefit Exchanges" to be established in every state by January 1, 2014, either by the state itself or by the Secretary of Health and Human Services (HHS). Exchanges will not be insurers, but will provide eligible individuals and small businesses with access to private health insurance plans. Generally, the plans offered through the exchanges will provide comprehensive coverage and meet all ACA market reforms, as applicable. One of the requirements that most exchange plans must meet is to provide a certain level of coverage generosity based on actuarial value. Each level of coverage generosity is designated according to a precious metal and corresponds to a specific actuarial value: Bronze (actuarial value of 60%), Silver (70%), Gold (80%), and Platinum (90%).

Chapter 3 – This document outlines the Department of Health and Human Services' (HHS) approach to implementing a Federally-facilitated Exchange (FFE) in any State where a State-based Exchange is not operating. In addition to describing our high-level operational approach, we discuss:

1. How States can partner with HHS to implement selected functions in an FFE,
2. Key policies organized by Exchange function, and
3. How HHS will consult with a variety of stakeholders to implement an FFE.

Subsequent guidance documents will include additional policy and operational details intended to inform State decision-making and preparation for Exchange participation, roles and responsibilities, and potential areas of collaboration.

In: Health Insurance Exchanges …
Editor: Edward J. Volpicelli
ISBN: 978-1-62417-367-7

Chapter 1

HEALTH INSURANCE EXCHANGES UNDER THE PATIENT PROTECTION AND AFFORDABLE CARE ACT (ACA)*

Bernadette Fernandez and Annie L. Mach

SUMMARY

The fundamental purpose of a health insurance exchange is to provide a structured marketplace for the sale and purchase of health insurance. The authority and responsibilities of an exchange may vary, depending on statutory or other requirements for its establishment and structure. The Patient Protection and Affordable Care Act (ACA, P.L. 111-148, as amended) requires health insurance exchanges to be established in every state by January 1, 2014. ACA provides certain requirements for the establishment of exchanges, while leaving other choices to be made by the states.

Qualified individuals and small businesses will be able to purchase private health insurance through exchanges. Issuers selling health insurance plans through an exchange will have to follow certain rules, such as meeting the private market reform requirements in ACA. While the fundamental purpose of the exchanges will be to facilitate the offer and purchase of health insurance, nothing in the law prohibits qualified individuals, qualified

---

* This is an edited, reformatted and augmented version of the Congressional Research Service Publication, CRS Report for Congress R42663, dated August 15, 2012.

employers, and insurance carriers from participating in the health insurance market outside of exchanges. Moreover, ACA explicitly states that enrollment in exchanges is voluntary and no individual may be compelled to enroll in exchange coverage.

Exchanges may be established either by the state itself as a "state exchange" or by the Secretary of Health and Human Services (HHS) as a "federally facilitated exchange." All exchanges are required to carry out many of the same functions and adhere to many of the same standards, although there are important differences between the types of exchanges. States will need to declare their intentions to establish their own exchanges by no later than November 16, 2012.

ACA and regulations require exchanges to carry out a number of different functions. The primary functions relate to determining eligibility and enrolling individuals in appropriate plans, plan management, consumer assistance and accountability, and financial management. ACA gives various federal agencies, primarily HHS, responsibilities relating to the general operation of exchanges. Federal agencies are generally responsible for promulgating regulations, creating criteria and systems, and awarding grants to states to help them create and implement exchanges.

A state that is approved to operate its own exchange has a number of operational decisions to make, including decisions related to organizational structure (governmental agency or a nonprofit entity); types of exchanges (separate individual and Small Business Health Options Program (SHOP) exchanges, or a merged exchange); collaboration (a state may independently operate an exchange or enter into contracts with other states); service area (a state may establish one or more subsidiary exchanges in the state if each exchange serves a geographically distinct area and meets certain size requirements); contracted services (an exchange may contract with certain entities to carry out one or more responsibilities of the exchange); and governance (governing board and standards of conduct).

In general, health plans offered through exchanges will provide comprehensive coverage and meet all applicable private market reforms specified in ACA. Most exchange plans will provide coverage for "essential health benefits," at minimum; be subject to certain limits on cost-sharing, including out-of-pocket costs; and meet one of four levels of plan generosity based on actuarial value. To make exchange coverage more affordable, certain individuals will receive premium assistance in the form of federal tax credits. Moreover, some recipients of premium credits may also receive subsidies toward cost-sharing expenses.

This report outlines the required minimum functions of exchanges, and explains how exchanges are expected to be established and administered under ACA. The coverage offered through exchanges is discussed, and the report concludes with a discussion of how exchanges will interact with selected other ACA provisions.

INTRODUCTION

A health insurance exchange is a structured marketplace for the sale and purchase of health insurance. "Customers" can include individuals and businesses. The insurance companies ("issuers") that choose to sell their products through an exchange may be required to comply with consumer protections, such as offering insurance to every qualified applicant. Exchanges, however, are not issuers; rather, exchanges contract with issuers who will make insurance products available for purchase through exchanges. Essentially, exchanges are designed to bring together buyers and sellers of insurance, with the goal of increasing access to coverage.

This rather broad definition allows for a great deal of latitude, and therefore variance, in the number and scope of responsibilities covered in a particular exchange. For example, the role of an exchange may be more or less administrative: facilitating the sale and purchase of health insurance. An administrative-only exchange may function similar to websites that allow individuals to find airline travel options and purchase tickets (e.g., Kayak). Such an approach does not necessarily change or establish standards for the products being sold (whether they are health plans or airline tickets), or limit the types of buyers and sellers participating in the exchange, beyond what already exists in the private market. An example of a minimalist health insurance exchange is the Utah Health Exchange. Essentially, Utah's exchange is an internet portal that is "designed to connect consumers to the information they need to make informed health care choices, and in the case of health insurance, to execute that choice electronically."[1]

At the other end of the spectrum, an exchange may have multiple functions beyond the role of insurance marketplace. For instance, an exchange may be responsible for implementing regulatory standards, such as requiring standardization of all products offered through it or imposing requirements on exchange participants. An exchange may be responsible for determining eligibility for exchange plans and government-provided subsidies. An example of a more regulatory-oriented exchange is the Health Connector ("Connector") in Massachusetts. Similar to Utah's exchange, the Connector provides an online tool to allow consumers and others to find commercial health insurance options available to them. In addition, the Connector also manages a publicly-subsidized coverage program for low-income state residents, and offers certificates to exempt individuals from the state's individual mandate, among other duties.[2]

An exchange may occupy a physical location and/or be virtual (i.e., performing its functions on the Internet). It may be governed by a public agency, a private entity, or a hybrid organization. The insurance options offered through an exchange may also vary across insurance markets[3] and plan types. Nonetheless, while the authority and responsibilities of an exchange may vary, its fundamental purpose is to provide a venue where insurance companies may sell their insurance products and purchasers can compare and choose from multiple options available to them. Thus an exchange allows for "one-stop shopping" with respect to health insurance.

The exchange concept was included in the Patient Protection and Affordable Care Act (ACA, P.L. 111-148, as amended), as a means to increase access to health insurance. While ACA places many restrictions on the design and function of exchanges, the law also leaves many operational decisions to the states. Such flexibility will likely lead to variation in exchange models across the states. For example, a state may decide to operate an exchange by itself, establish an exchange in partnership with the federal government, or leave this work entirely to the federal government. The deadlines for making such complex decisions are approaching quickly. By November 16, 2012, states must declare whether or not they will assume the responsibility for establishing exchanges. The initial open enrollment period will begin on October 1, 2013, and exchanges are to be operational and offering coverage on January 1, 2014.

This report looks at the requirements for exchanges established in ACA and provides information on the requirements and choices available to states for the establishment, functions, financial responsibilities, and coverage of the ACA exchanges. It also includes a brief discussion of the interactions between exchanges and other provisions in the law.

ACA Exchanges

ACA intends exchanges to be marketplaces where qualified individuals and small businesses can "shop" for private health insurance coverage.[4] The coverage offered through exchanges will be comprehensive[5] and meet all applicable private market reforms[6] specified in ACA. Such plans offered through the exchanges will be certified as "qualified health plans" or QHPs.[7]

ACA explicitly states that enrollment in exchanges is voluntary and no individual may be compelled to enroll in exchange coverage.[8] While the main purpose of the exchanges will be to facilitate the offer and purchase of health insurance, nothing in the ACA prohibits qualified individuals, qualified small businesses, and insurance carriers from participating in the health insurance market outside of exchanges.[9]

For individuals seeking coverage, exchanges will not only create marketplaces where qualified individuals can purchase QHPs in the nongroup (individual) market, but exchanges will also assist individuals with obtaining federally-subsidized premium and cost-sharing assistance to help low to middle income individuals offset the cost of both purchasing and using health insurance. Exchanges will also screen individuals for eligibility for certain public insurance programs (e.g., Medicaid) and connect them with appropriate agencies.

Small businesses seeking coverage for their employees will be able to use the small business health options program (SHOP) exchange. The SHOP exchange is designed to assist qualified small employers and their employees with the purchase of QHPs offered in the small group market. Qualified small employers will be able to select QHPs available in the SHOP to offer to their employees, and they will be able to set the amount they will contribute to QHP premiums.

ACA requires exchanges to be established in every state by January 1, 2014. Exchanges must be established by the state itself or by the Secretary of Health and Human Services (HHS),[10] and they must carry out the general functions described above for both individuals and small businesses. Additionally, exchanges will be expected to perform a number of other functions relating to managing the QHPs offered through the exchanges and assisting individuals and small businesses in accessing and obtaining coverage.

ESTABLISHMENT OF ACA EXCHANGES

ACA provides general direction regarding the establishment and administration of an exchange. ACA is supplemented by the final regulation on the establishment of exchanges and other guidance produced by federal agencies, particularly HHS.[11] Taken together, these documents set forth some requirements and minimum standards that various stakeholders – including consumers, states, issuers, and employers – must meet to be part of or to participate in an exchange.

One factor that could influence a number of determinations related to how an exchange is implemented is whether the exchange is established by a state or HHS. States have the option of establishing their own exchanges ("state exchange") as a governmental agency or a non-profit entity. If a state wants to operate its own exchange beginning January 1, 2014, it must submit required documents no later than November 16, 2012 for the exchange to be approved by HHS by January 1, 2013.[12]

If a state's exchange is not approved, or if a state chooses not to establish its own exchange, the HHS Secretary has the authority to establish and operate an exchange in that state directly, or through an agreement with a non-profit entity.[13] In a "federally-facilitated exchange," HHS will carry out all functions of the exchange and have authority over the exchange. HHS gives states the option to enter into a hybrid type of exchange – somewhere between a state exchange and a federally-facilitated exchange. This option is referred to as a "partnership" with a federally-facilitated exchange, whereby certain state-designed and operated functions are combined with federally-designed and operated functions. While HHS and states share responsibility for carrying out functions in partnerships within federally-facilitated exchanges, HHS retains authority over these exchanges.[14]

Regardless of whether an exchange is established by a state or the federal government, the initial open enrollment period for an exchange will be October 1, 2013 through March 31, 2014. Exchanges must begin offering coverage to qualified individuals and small businesses on January 1, 2014.[15]

State Exchanges

The HHS Secretary must approve the operation of a state exchange if it meets the following standards:

- the exchange is able to carry out the required functions of the exchange as established in the law and regulation, which include making QHPs available to qualified individuals and qualified employers;
- the exchange is capable of carrying out the information reporting requirements related to sharing information with the federal

government in order to determine an individual's eligibility for a premium tax credit;[16] and
- either the entire geographic area of the state is covered in the exchange or the state has established multiple exchanges that cover the entire geographic area of the state.[17]

A state exchange is responsible for creating and implementing its structure and governing system according to the guidelines outlined in the statute and regulations, as discussed below.

Operational Structure of a State Exchange

A state that is approved to establish its own exchange has a number of decisions to make regarding the exchange's operational structure. A state must determine whether its exchange will be a governmental agency or a non-profit established by the state. The terms "governmental" and "non-profit established by the state," have not been defined; instead, it seems these terms are subject to state interpretation.[18]

A state can choose to independently operate an exchange, or a state can enter into contracts with other states (regardless of whether the states are contiguous) to operate a regional exchange.[19] States can also establish one or more subsidiary exchanges in the state if each exchange serves a geographically distinct area and if the area served by each exchange meets the geographic size requirement established in the law.[20] In other words, while states have a great deal of leeway in establishing how the exchange is divided up geographically, they must serve the entire population in their state. Furthermore, regional exchanges and subsidiary exchanges must meet all exchange requirements.

A state exchange must operate both the individual and SHOP exchanges, but a state can either merge the exchanges and operate both under the same administrative and governance structures, or elect to create separate administrative and governance structures for the individual and SHOP exchanges.[21] Additionally, regional and subsidiary exchanges must perform the functions of a SHOP exchange. If an exchange chooses to operate an individual exchange and a SHOP exchange under two different governance and administrative structures, a SHOP exchange must cover the same geographic area as the regional or subsidiary individual exchange.[22]

States also have the authority to allow a state exchange to contract with the entities described below to carry out one or more responsibilities of the exchange.[23] States can grant this authority to state exchanges independent of whether an exchange is a governmental agency or a non-profit established by the state. For example, a state exchange that is a non-profit established by the state could contract with a state agency that meets the criteria below to carry out certain consumer assistance functions for the exchange.

A state exchange may contract with

- an entity, including a state agency other than a Medicaid agency, incorporated under and subject to the laws of at least one state, that has demonstrated experience on a state or regional basis in the individual and small group health insurance markets and in benefits coverage, but is not an issuer; and/or
- a state Medicaid agency.

Governance of a State Exchange

Generally, a state exchange must have a governing board that meets certain requirements; the board must[24]

- be administered under a publicly-adopted operating charter or by-laws;
- hold regular meetings that are open to the public and announced in advance;
- ensure that the board's membership includes at least one voting member who is a consumer representative and is not made up of a majority of voting representatives with conflicts of interest (e.g., representatives of issuers); and
- ensure that a majority of the voting members on its governing board have relevant experience in the health care field (e.g., in health benefits administration, or in public health).

In addition, a state exchange is required to have in place and make publicly available a set of governance principles that include ethics, conflict of interest standards, transparency and accounting standards, and standards related to disclosure of financial interests. A state exchange must also implement procedures as to how members of the governing board will disclose any financial interests. The state exchange's governance principles are subject to periodic review by HHS.[25]

Federally Facilitated Exchange

If a state chooses not to operate its own exchange, or if a state does not have approval to operate its own exchange as of January 1, 2013, the HHS Secretary is required to establish a "federally-facilitated exchange" in the state.[26] A federally-facilitated exchange can be implemented by HHS alone, or a state can enter into a "partnership" with a federally-facilitated exchange, combining state-designed and operated functions with federally-designed and operated functions.[27] Partnerships are considered a "subset" of federally-facilitated exchanges, indicating that HHS has authority over partnerships in federally-facilitated exchanges.[28]

The final rule on the establishment of exchanges does not include provisions specific to federally-facilitated exchanges (instead saying that information for these exchanges will be provided in future guidance). However, the final rule does indicate that federally-facilitated exchanges are required to carry-out many of the same functions as state exchanges. Additionally, federally-facilitated exchanges and state exchanges must adhere to many of the same standards outlined in ACA and the final rule. For example, state exchanges and federally-facilitated exchanges are both required to offer the same tools to help consumers access an exchange and assess their plan options through an exchange.

Although there are no specific regulations related to federally-facilitated exchanges, HHS has published some *guidance*, which generally describes how HHS will operate federally-facilitated exchanges within the framework established by ACA and the final rule.[29] This guidance includes information such as descriptions of a state's potential responsibilities if the state decides to enter into a partnership with a federally-facilitated exchange. Further guidance related to federally-facilitated exchanges is expected.

What Exchanges Do

Exchanges are required to carry out a number of different functions, including determining eligibility and enrolling individuals in appropriate plans; conducting plan management activities; assisting consumers, ensuring plan accountability; and providing financial management.[30] These functions are not necessarily exhaustive of exchange responsibilities; rather, this section is intended to provide a general overview of an exchange's responsibilities. Unless otherwise noted, both state and federally-facilitated exchanges are required to carry out the functions described in this section. Additionally, some responsibilities may be different for individual exchanges and SHOP exchanges, so the following discussion provides information for both.

Eligibility and Enrollment

Exchanges are responsible for a variety of functions related to determining an applicant's eligibility (whether an individual's or an employer's) for various plans/programs and for enrolling eligible applicants into those plans/ programs. With these eligibility and enrollment responsibilities come the responsibility to verify the information received from applicants and to re-determine eligibility as necessary. An exchange's responsibilities to determine eligibility and to enroll eligible individuals are different, but related, for the individual exchange and the SHOP exchange (for small business employees).

Individual Exchange

ACA intends to create a seamless eligibility and enrollment process for individuals seeking health insurance coverage in the nongroup market and/or through public programs (e.g., Medicaid). The process would allow individuals to fill out a single application that collects the information necessary to screen the individual for multiple types of coverage and financial assistance. The process would then facilitate the enrollment of the individual in the appropriate plan/program.

An individual exchange is expected to implement this streamlined process.[31] An individual exchange will determine an applicant's eligibility for enrollment in a QHP.[32] Additionally, an individual exchange will screen individuals for eligibility for insurance affordability programs (IAP),[33] which include Medicaid, the State Children's Health Insurance Program (CHIP), the Basic Health Program (BHP),[34] advanced payment of premium tax credits, and cost-sharing reductions.

To determine eligibility, an individual exchange must use a single, streamlined application to collect information from an applicant and verify that information according to procedures identified in regulation. For example, an individual exchange is expected to verify an applicant's social security number by transmitting the number to HHS, which will consult the Social Security Administration and the Department of Homeland Security, as needed, to verify the number.[35] An individual exchange is expected to re-determine an enrollee's eligibility if the individual exchange receives and verifies new information relating to the enrollee.

This information can come from the enrollee, as enrollees are required to report any change with respect to eligibility standards within 30 days of the change, or it can come from information the individual exchange finds through its required periodic examination of available information that might affect eligibility (e.g., whether an enrollee has died). An individual exchange is also expected to re-determine or re-assess the eligibility of all enrollees on an annual basis. However, re-determinations and re-assessments due to changes in status do not fully satisfy the requirement for annual re-determinations and re-assessments.[36]

The final rule on exchange establishment gives exchanges some flexibility related to determining eligibility for QHPs and IAPs. This flexibility is discussed below, where appropriate.

Eligibility for Enrollment in a QHP

An individual exchange is required to determine an applicant's eligibility for enrollment in a QHP. If an applicant is determined eligible for a QHP, the individual exchange is expected to facilitate the applicant's enrollment into the QHP selected by the individual. Table 1 shows the criteria an individual exchange must use to determine eligibility for enrollment in a QHP.

Table 1. Criteria for Determining Eligibility for Enrollment in a QHP

An individual exchange must determine an applicant eligible for a QHP if the applicant meets the following criteria:	
Enrollment in a QHP	• Citizen, national, or noncitizen who is lawfully present in the United States[a] • Not incarcerated, other than pending the disposition of charges • Meets applicable state residency standards

Source: CRS analysis of ACA (as amended) and 77 *Federal Register* 18310, March 27, 2012.

a. Only lawful residents may obtain exchange coverage; unauthorized aliens will be prohibited from obtaining coverage through an exchange, even if they could pay the entire premium without a subsidy.

Eligibility for Premium Tax Credits and Cost-Sharing Subsidies

Certain individuals who purchase a QHP through an individual exchange will be eligible for financial assistance to help them off-set the cost of the coverage and to defray some costs associated with using health services.

ACA provides assistance, for the purchase of exchange coverage, in the form of premium tax credits. (A tax credit is a reduction that is applied to the amount an individual (or family) owes, if any, when filing income taxes.) Premium tax credits are advanceable, meaning instead of having to wait until after the end of the tax year to receive the credit, the individual may receive the payments in advance to coincide with when insurance premiums are due (usually on a monthly basis).

In addition to the premium tax credits, ACA provides cost-sharing subsides to certain individuals to help them pay costs related to the use of health services. (Cost-sharing generally refers to costs that an individual must pay when using services that are covered under the health plan that the person is enrolled in; common forms of cost-sharing include copayments and deductibles.)

Both premium tax credits and cost-sharing subsidies are discussed later in this report under the section "Cost Assistance."

Because the premium tax credits are advanceable, it will be necessary to determine an individual's eligibility for the credits at the time the individual applies for coverage through an exchange. In regard to advanced payment of premium tax credits, an individual exchange may either *determine* an applicant's eligibility directly or *implement a determination* of eligibility made by HHS.[37]

Determining eligibility directly is similar to determining eligibility for QHPs; the individual exchange reviews an applicant's information and makes a determination of eligibility. If an individual exchange chooses to determine an applicant's eligibility for advance payment of premium tax credits, the exchange must calculate the amount of the advance payment in accordance with section 36B of the Internal Revenue Code. An individual exchange may only provide the advance payment if the applicant meets the eligibility criteria (see Table 2).

Similarly, an individual exchange may either directly determine eligibility for cost-sharing subsidies, or it may implement a determination made by HHS. If an individual exchange chooses to determine an applicant's eligibility for cost-sharing subsidies, the exchange must do so according to the criteria outlined in Table 2.

If an individual exchange decides *not* to directly determine eligibility for advanced payment of premium tax credits or *not* to directly determine eligibility for cost-sharing subsidies but rather implements HHS determinations, then an individual exchange is expected to transmit all collected and verified information to HHS. The individual exchange does not make a recommendation in this process; rather, the individual exchange shares information with HHS and then is expected to adhere to the determination of eligibility made by HHS.[38]

Table 2. Criteria for Determining Eligibility for Subsidies Through an Exchange

An exchange or HHS may determine an applicant eligible for the subsidies below according to the following criteria:	

Advanced payment of premium tax credits	• Meets the criteria for eligibility for enrollment in a QHP through an exchange[a]
	• Not eligible for minimum essential coverage (other than through the individual health insurance market)[b]
	• Is part of a tax-filing unit
	• Is enrolled in a QHP offered through an exchange
	• Has household income that either
	  • is between 100% and 400% FPL; or
	  • is not greater than 100% FPL and is an alien lawfully present (but not eligible for Medicaid because of duration of U.S. residency)[c]

Cost-sharing subsidies	• Meets the criteria for eligibility for enrollment in a QHP through an exchange • Meets the criteria for eligibility for advance payment of premium tax credits • Is enrolled in a silver plan through an exchange[d] • Has household income between 100% and 400% FPL[e]

Source: CRS analysis of ACA (as amended) and 77 *Federal Register* 18310, March 27, 2012.

a. These criteria are detailed in **Table 1**.

b. The definition of minimum essential coverage is discussed in CRS Report R41331, *Individual Mandate and Related Information Requirements under ACA*, by Janemarie Mulvey and Hinda Chaikind.

c. The Personal Responsibility and Work Opportunity Reconciliation Act of 1996 (P.L. 104-193) determined that most individuals who are not citizens but are lawfully present in the United States are barred from Medicaid for the first five years that they are in the United States.

d. A description of the different tiers of coverage offered through an exchange is included in the "Coverage Levels and Benefits" section of this report.

e. The cost-sharing subsidies reduces the annual caps on out-of-pocket expenses for individuals with income between 100% and 400% FPL. Additionally, ACA requires QHP issuers to further reduce cost-sharing requirements for individuals with income between 100% and 250% FPL. For more information, see CRS Report R41137, *Health Insurance Premium Credits in the Patient Protection and Affordable Care Act (ACA)*, by Bernadette Fernandez and Thomas Gabe.

Table 3. Criteria for Determining or Assessing Eligibility for Enrollment in Medicaid and CHIP

An individual exchange may determine an applicant eligible or assess an applicant's eligibility for Medicaid and CHIP according to the following criteria:		
	Determination	**Assessment**
Enrollment in Medicaid	• Meets the non-financial criteria for Medicaid for populations whose eligibility is based on modified adjusted gross income (MAGI)[a] • Has a household income that is at or below the applicable Medicaid MAGI- based income standard • Is either a pregnant woman, under age 19, a parent or caretaker of a dependent child, or is under age 65 and not entitled to or enrolled in Medicare Parts A or B	• Makes the assessment based on the applicable Medicaid MAGI-based income standards and citizenship and immigration status, using verification rules and procedures consistent with Medicaid statute, regardless of how such standards are implemented by the state Medicaid agency • Must adhere to state Medicaid agency's final determination of applicant's eligibility
Enrollment in CHIP	• Meets the requirements for children to enroll in CHIP[b] • Has a household income at or below the applicable CHIP MAGI-based income standard	• Makes the assessment based on the applicable CHIP MAGI- based income standards and citizenship and immigration status, using verification rules and procedures consistent with CHIP statute, regardless of how such standards are implemented by the state CHIP agency • Must adhere to state CHIP agency's final determination of applicant's eligibility

Source: CRS analysis of ACA (as amended) and 77 *Federal Register* 18310, March 27, 2012.

a. For information about populations whose Medicaid eligibility is, in part, based on MAGI-based income, see CRS Report R41210, *Medicaid and the State Children's Health Insurance Program (CHIP) Provisions in ACA: Summary and Timeline*, by Evelyne P. Baumrucker et al.

b. For more information about children's eligibility for CHIP, see CRS Report R40444, *State Children's Health Insurance Program (CHIP): A Brief Overview*, by Elicia J. Herz and Evelyne P. Baumrucker.

Eligibility for Medicaid and CHIP

An individual exchange may either *determine* or *assess* an applicant's eligibility for enrollment in Medicaid and/or CHIP. If an individual exchange chooses to *determine* eligibility for Medicaid and/or CHIP, then the individual exchange is also responsible for the enrollment of eligible applicants. Once an applicant has been determined eligible, the individual exchange must transmit the applicant's information to the state Medicaid or CHIP agency, thus effectuating enrollment.

An individual exchange may choose to only *assess* eligibility for Medicaid/CHIP. If an applicant is assessed eligible for a program the individual exchange is required to transmit all collected and verified information to the state Medicaid or CHIP agency to enable the agency to make a final determination of the applicant's eligibility. In this case, the exchange is only making a recommendation and sharing information with the appropriate agency; it is not responsible for making a final determination of eligibility. The individual exchange is expected to adhere to the final determination made by the agency.

Table 3 shows criteria an individual exchange must use to determine or assess eligibility for enrollment in Medicaid and CHIP.[39]

Eligibility for Enrollment in a BHP

The Basic Health Program (BHP) is a health insurance program for low-income individuals who are not eligible for Medicaid, and is offered in lieu of eligible individuals obtaining coverage through an exchange. States have the option to implement the BHP, and therefore, exchanges will interact with BHPs in only those states that choose to implement a BHP.

If a state chooses to establish a BHP, an individual exchange is expected to *determine* an applicant's eligibility for a BHP, and facilitate the applicant's enrollment in the program. Table 4 shows the criteria an individual exchange must use to determine eligibility for enrollment in a BHP.

SHOP Exchange

As the exchange for small businesses, the SHOP has responsibilities similar to the individual exchange in that the SHOP is also responsible for collecting and verifying information from employers and employees (both considered applicants), determining eligibility, and facilitating enrollment. An employer and each of its employees seeking coverage must submit an application to the SHOP. The SHOP must process the applications, and if the employer and employees are determined eligible, the SHOP must facilitate the enrollment of qualified employees into QHPs offered through the SHOP.

A qualified employee is an employee who receives an offer of coverage from a qualified employer. A qualified employer is a small group employer[40] that elects to make, at a minimum, all full-time employees eligible for one or more QHPs offered in the small group market through an exchange, and has its principal business in the exchange service area or offers coverage to each eligible employee through the SHOP serving the employee's worksite.[41]

The SHOP is required to verify applicants' eligibility as outlined in regulation.[42] The SHOP must permit an employer to purchase coverage for employees at any time during the year, but the employer's plan must consist of a 12-month period beginning with the employer's effective date of coverage. Employees must adhere to annual open enrollment periods as determined by the SHOP, with special allowances for newly qualified employees.

Employers are not required to offer all the plans in an exchange to their employees. The SHOP must allow an employer to limit the selection of plans.[43]

Plan Management Responsibilities

Exchanges are required to ensure that QHPs are certified.[44] An exchange may certify a plan as a QHP if the plan meets the required minimum criteria and if the exchange determines that it is in the best interest of qualified individuals and employers to have such a plan available.[45] The minimum certification criteria outlined in ACA and further defined through regulation include requirements related to marketing, choice of providers, plan networks, accreditation,[46] and other features.[47]

In addition to certifying QHPs, an exchange must establish processes for recertification and decertification of QHPs. The recertification process, at a minimum, must include a review of the general certification criteria and must be completed on or before September 15 of the applicable calendar year.

The decertification process must, at a minimum, include the following requirements: the ability for an exchange to decertify a plan at any time if the exchange determines that the QHP no longer meets the certification requirements; an exchange must establish a process for the appeal of a decertification; and an exchange must provide a notice of the decertification to all affected parties, including the QHP issuer, the exchange enrollees, HHS, and the state insurance department.

Table 4. Criteria for Determining Eligibility for Enrollment in a BHP

An individual exchange must determine an applicant eligible for a BHP if the applicant meets the following criteria:	

Enrollment in the Basic Health Program (BHP)	• Resident of a state and not eligible for the state's Medicaid program
	• Not eligible for minimum essential coverage or is eligible for employer-sponsored insurance (ESI) that is not affordable[a]
	• Has not attained age 65 at the beginning of the plan year
	• Has household income that either
	  • exceeds 133% of the federal poverty level (FPL) but does not exceed 200% FPL; or
	  • is not greater than 133% FPL and is an alien lawfully present (but not eligible for Medicaid because of duration of U.S. residency)[b]

Source: CRS analysis of ACA (as amended) and 77 *Federal Register* 18310, March 27, 2012.

a. The definition of minimum essential coverage is discussed in CRS Report R41331, *Individual Mandate and Related Information Requirements under ACA*, by Janemarie Mulvey and Hinda Chaikind. ACA considers employer coverage "unaffordable" if the employee's contribution toward the employer's lowest-cost self-only premium exceeds 9.5% of household income.

b. The Personal Responsibility and Work Opportunity Reconciliation Act of 1996 (P.L. 104-193) determined that most individuals who are not citizens but are lawfully present in the United States are barred from Medicaid for the first five years that they are in the United States.

An exchange has additional plan management functions. For example, the exchange must require plans seeking certification as QHPs to submit justification for premium increases before it takes effect, and the plans will have to post the information about their premium increases on their websites.[48] Also, the HHS Secretary is required to create a system that rates QHPs on the basis of relative quality and price. An exchange is expected to assign a rating to each QHP according to the HHS Secretary's criteria and provide the quality rating information through its website.[49]

Consumer Assistance and Accountability

Exchanges have a number of responsibilities related to assisting consumers in accessing and obtaining coverage, including providing tools to help consumers access the exchange, helping consumers determine which plan or program to enroll in, and helping consumers determine their potential financial responsibility for a QHP offered through an exchange.[50] Additionally, exchanges are expected to adhere to accountability practices to increase an exchange's transparency.

The following are some of an exchange's responsibilities related to assisting consumers and being accountable to stakeholders, including consumers. An exchange must

- Provide for operation of a toll-free telephone hotline that addresses the needs of consumers requesting assistance and informs individuals with disabilities and limited English proficiency of the availability of services to assist them.
- Maintain a website which, among other things, provides standardized comparative information on each QHP available through the exchange and allows qualified individuals to select a QHP in which to enroll.[51]
- Make available an electronic calculator (through its website) that facilitates the comparison of available QHPs (including the impact of any advance payments of tax credits and cost-sharing subsidies in the individual exchange and the impact of any employer contribution in the SHOP exchange).
- Conduct outreach and education activities that will educate consumers about the exchange and insurance affordability programs (IAPs) to encourage participation.[52]
- Establish a Navigator program with grants to eligible individuals and entities to provide information about the exchange and help individuals select a QHP. Navigators are also required to conduct activities to raise awareness of an exchange.[53]
- Include results on its website from the Secretary's survey on enrollee satisfaction with the QHPs offered through the exchange, in a manner that allows for easy comparisons of enrollee satisfaction levels.[54]
- Regularly consult with stakeholders regarding the accessibility and administration of an exchange. These stakeholders include enrollees of QHPs; individuals and entities with experience in facilitating enrollment in health insurance coverage; advocates for hard to reach populations (e.g., individuals with substance abuse problems); small businesses, large employers, and self-employed individuals; state Medicaid and CHIP agencies; federally-recognized Tribes; public health experts; issuers; and health insurance agents and brokers.[55]

- Share financial information on its website, regarding: any regulatory fees or other payments required by the exchange; administrative costs of the exchange; and monies lost to waste, fraud, and abuse.[56]
- Determine the role of agents and brokers in the exchange. An exchange may allow agents and brokers to be Navigators, provided they otherwise meet the Navigator eligibility criteria.[57] An exchange may also allow agents and brokers to enroll individuals and employers in QHPs offered through an exchange if the agents and brokers meet certain requirements.[58]

ACA Risk Mitigation Programs

Exchanges are expected to deal with the potential for adverse selection. Adverse selection occurs when a large number of individuals who expect or plan for high use of health services enroll in more generous and often more expensive health plans (i.e., a woman who plans to become pregnant switches from a plan with less generous maternity benefits to a plan with more generous maternity benefits), while simultaneously individuals who expect or plan for low use of health services enroll in more modest plans, both in terms of price and benefits. Adverse selection can lead to health plans that have risk pools with a large number of high-cost individuals, which can lead to higher costs for individuals in the pool, and in extreme instances, possible dissolution of the pool due to an increasingly expensive risk pool.

ACA establishes three risk programs to help mitigate the potential impact of adverse selection: reinsurance, risk corridors, and risk adjustment. The first two programs are temporary and are intended to provide some protection against risk in the short term before a full risk adjustment program can be developed. None of the programs are specific to exchanges; rather, they are tools that can be used both inside and outside the exchanges to mitigate the impact of adverse selection. For more information about ACA's risk programs, see Appendix B.

Financial Management

Exchanges are responsible for financial management and are expected to be self-sustaining by 2015. They have been given authority to generate funding to support their operations; however, while the law and regulation describe this authority, neither specify how an exchange may or may not generate funding.[59] An example provided in regulation is that exchanges could charge participating issuers assessments or user fees.[60]

Exchanges are expected to play a role in collecting premiums and distributing the premiums to issuers. ACA requires exchanges to perform certain functions relating to financial oversight and integrity, including keeping an accurate accounting of all financial activities and submitting a report annually to the HHS Secretary concerning such accountings. Exchanges are also required to cooperate with investigations into the affairs of exchanges, conducted by the HHS Secretary in coordination with HHS Inspector General.[61]

Federal Responsibilities for Establishment and Administration of All Exchanges

ACA requires federal agencies, primarily HHS, to oversee the exchanges, thus carrying out a number of responsibilities related to the establishment and administration of exchanges. Many of these responsibilities require federal agencies to create systems and criteria. For example, the HHS Secretary is required to develop the minimum criteria an exchange will use to certify QHPs to be offered through an exchange.[62] The HHS Secretary is also required to grant financial awards to states to be used to establish exchanges.

Federal Oversight

Federal agencies, primarily HHS, have oversight and other responsibilities for exchanges. These responsibilities not only relate to the general operation of the exchange, but they also relate to how an exchange is expected to share information and coordinate its duties with federal agencies.

It is beyond the scope of this report to detail all of the responsibilities ACA gives to federal agencies;[63] however, the following are general examples of duties required of federal agencies. Other examples are included in this report, where appropriate.

- The HHS Secretary is required to promulgate regulations relating to, among other things, setting standards for the establishment and operation of exchanges, the offering of QHPs through exchanges, and the establishment of the reinsurance and risk adjustment programs established by ACA.[64]

- The HHS Secretary is expected to coordinate efforts between the exchange and other federal agencies (such as the Social Security Administration) to verify information collected by the exchange from applicants and related to eligibility for the exchange and other programs (e.g., premium tax credits).[65]
- The HHS Secretary is expected, through consultation with other entities (such as the National Association of Insurance Commissioners), to develop and maintain tools and set minimum standards for tools that exchanges may use to assist consumers with accessing the exchange.[66]

Federal Financial Assistance

While exchanges are expected to be self-sufficient by 2015, there is some limited federal assistance provided to states to help them as they develop their exchanges.[67] ACA requires the HHS Secretary to award planning and establishment grants to states for the purposes of activities related to establishing exchanges.[68] ACA gives the HHS Secretary the authority to determine the amount of the grants and to renew the grants if a state is making sufficient progress toward establishing an exchange. No planning and establishment grant may be awarded after December 31, 2014.[69]

Planning grants were given to 49 states and the District of Columbia.[70] These grants of up to $1 million each were intended to provide resources to states to help them conduct research and planning related to establishing exchanges. Establishment grants have also been awarded to a number of states. Level one establishment grants are annual awards to states who are still in the initial phases of developing exchanges, and level two establishment grants are multi-year awards intended to assist states that have made significant progress in implementation of exchanges. To date, 34 states and the District of Columbia have received level one grants, and two states have received level two grants.[71] In total, the states and the District of Columbia have received more than $856 million in establishment grants.[72]

The HHS Secretary is also required to award grants to eligible entities to help them develop and adapt technology systems to be used by an exchange to determine eligibility and process enrollment.[73] These "early innovator" grants were given to seven entities to help them design and implement the information technology infrastructure needed to operate an exchange.[74] The grants were awarded to entities that have "demonstrated their technical expertise and ability to develop these IT systems on a fast track schedule, and their willingness to share design and implementation solutions with other states."[75] The seven entities combined have received more than $249 million in early innovator grants.[76]

COVERAGE OFFERED THROUGH THE EXCHANGES

Most private health insurance plans sold through exchanges must include a comprehensive set of benefits. The law specifies standards for the types and levels of coverage that can be offered through exchanges.

Coverage Levels and Benefits

Generally, exchange plans must (1) cover "essential health benefits" (EHBs), at a minimum; (2) limit cost-sharing, including out-of-pocket costs; and (3) provide coverage that meets one of four levels of plan generosity based on actuarial value (defined below).[77] These requirements will become effective beginning in 2014, to dovetail with the establishment of exchanges. The following discusses them in greater detail.

Essential Health Benefits

ACA does not explicitly list the benefits that comprise essential health benefits (EHBs). Instead, the law identifies 10 broad benefit categories which must be included in EHBs, at a minimum:

- ambulatory patient services;
- emergency services;
- hospitalization;
- maternity and newborn care;
- mental health and substance use disorder services, including behavioral health treatment;
- prescription drugs;
- rehabilitative and habilitative services and devices;
- laboratory services;

- preventive and wellness and chronic disease management; and
- pediatric services, including oral and vision care.

States may impose additional benefit mandates beyond what is required under EHBs. However, any state that requires health plans to offer benefits beyond EHBs must assume the total cost of providing those additional benefits, for all the plans, and regardless of whether or not an individual is receiving any financial assistance with premiums or cost-sharing. The state must make payments either directly to the individuals enrolled in health plans affected by the state benefit mandates, or to such plans on behalf of enrolled individuals.[78]

The bulk of the responsibility for defining EHBs is given to the HHS Secretary, who must then notify the public and provide the opportunity for comment. The HHS Secretary has certain guidelines that must be followed in developing the EHBs, including ensuring that the scope of EHBs is equal to the scope of benefits under a "typical" employer-provided health plan (as certified by the Chief Actuary of the Centers for Medicare & Medicaid Services), and that EHBs meet equity and other standards specified in the law. To assist the HHS Secretary in this determination, the law requires the Secretary of the Department of Labor (Labor) to conduct a survey of employer-provided health coverage.[79]

ACA did not specify a deadline for when the Secretary is required to define EHBs. To date, HHS has not issued regulations defining EHBs. Instead, HHS published a bulletin which stated that "EHB be defined by a benchmark plan selected by each State."[80] HHS identified four benchmark plan types that a state could use for the purpose of defining EHBs in that state:

- one of the three largest plans in the state's small group health insurance market;[81]
- one of the three largest state employees health benefits plans;
- one of the three largest national plans offered through the Federal Employees Health Benefits Program (FEHBP); or
- the largest commercial non-Medicaid health maintenance organization in the state.

To assist states in this effort, HHS conducted studies that identified the largest plans (by enrollment) for several of the benchmark plan types listed above, and documented the prevalence of certain benefits in health plans that are currently offered.[82] HHS found that the largest national FEHBP plan, by far, is offered through Blue Cross and Blue Shield; and while small group plans vary by state, the ones with the largest enrollment generally are offered by large, commercial insurance carriers.

Cost-Sharing Requirements

Cost-sharing includes deductibles and co-payments for services rendered. ACA limits the amount of cost-sharing that exchange plans generally may impose on enrolled individuals. These cost-sharing limits prohibit

- any deductible applicable to preventive health services;
- deductibles, in small group health plans, that are greater than $2,000 for self-only coverage, or $4,000 for any other coverage in 2014 (annually adjusted thereafter);[83] and
- annual cost-sharing limits that exceed existing limits specified in the tax code, relating to certain high deductible health plans.[84]

Levels of Plan Generosity

Health plans that provide the essential health benefits package must tailor cost-sharing to meet one of four levels of generosity, based on actuarial value.[85]

Actuarial value (AV) is a summary measure of a plan's generosity, expressed as the percentage of medical expenses estimated to be paid by the issuer for a standard population and set of allowed charges. In other words, AV reflects the relative share of cost-sharing that may be imposed. In general, the lower the AV, the greater the cost-sharing, on average.[86]

Each level of plan generosity is designated according to a precious metal and corresponds to a specific actuarial value:

Levels	Actuarial Value
Bronze	60%
Silver	70%
Gold	80%
Platinum	90%

While the term actuarial value may imply a high level of precision,

> actuarial analysis is inherently an estimation process and hence is somewhat inexact. Actuarial value estimates will vary by the data sources, projection methods, and assumptions used, and there may be a reasonable range of appropriate methods and assumptions used to develop these estimates.[87]

Given this, ACA requires the HHS Secretary to promulgate regulations regarding the determination of the levels of plan generosity. The determination will be based on a benefit package consisting of essential health benefits and a standard population.

To date, HHS issued a bulletin that described its proposed definition for actuarial value and solicited comments. In the bulletin, HHS proposes to use a standard data set based on a countrywide standard population, with the option for individual states to "develop State standard populations based on State claims data."[88]

Exchange Health Plans

Exchanges will offer several types of health plans, as specified in statute and regulation. Exchange plans will provide a comprehensive set of covered benefits (i.e., the essential health benefits), except for stand-alone dental plans (which will have to meet a narrow set of benefit requirements). While most of these comprehensive plans will be available to any individual or employer who is qualified to enroll in exchanges (such as multi-state QHPs and CO-OP QHPs),[89] some plans will be available only to specific subpopulations (child-only QHPs and catastrophic QHPs).[90] Finally, some plans offered in exchanges may also be offered outside of exchanges.[91]

Qualified Health Plans

In general, exchanges will offer comprehensive coverage that meets the standards to be certified as "qualified health plans" (QHPs),[92] provided it meets requirements related to marketing, choice of providers, plan networks, and other features, or is recognized by each exchange through which such plan is offered.[93] In addition, all QHPs are required to comply with benefit, cost-sharing and generosity components of the essential health benefits package (described above). In addition to qualified health plans, exchanges will also offer multi-state QHPs, child-only QHPs, and CO-OP QHPs (described below).

An issuer of QHPs must be licensed and in good standing with each state in which it offers coverage; must offer at least one QHP each providing silver and gold levels of coverage; and must comply with regulations applicable to exchanges. An issuer may offer QHPs outside of exchanges as well as inside, but the premiums would have to be the same, even if the QHP is sold through an insurance agent.[94]

Multi-state Qualified Health Plans

Multi-state qualified health plans are designed to offer nationally available QHPs, so that individuals and small businesses will all have access to these plans, regardless of where they live. The Director of the Office of Personnel Management (OPM) will enter into contracts with issuers to offer at least two multi-state qualified health plans (MSQHPs) ultimately through every exchange in all the states.[95] Any individual eligible to purchase insurance through the exchange may enroll in an MSQHP. Enrollment is voluntary, and individuals may be eligible for premium credits and cost-sharing assistance.

Each contract for an MSQHP will be for at least one year and can be automatically renewed if neither party provides notice to terminate. At least one contract will be with a nonprofit entity, and at least one contract cannot provide coverage for abortion services.[96] The OPM Director will enter into a contract with an issuer if the issuer offers the plan in at least 60% of states in the first year, at least 70% in the second year, at least 85% in the third year, and in all states thereafter.

An issuer offering a MSQHP must meet certain requirements and adhere to certain policies. For example, an issuer offering a MSQHP must meet the requirements in every state's exchange, offer a uniform benefits package in each state consisting of the essential health benefits, and comply with the minimum standards prescribed for carriers offering health benefits plans under the Federal Employees Health Benefits Program (FEHBP).[97] However, unlike other QHPs offered through an exchange, which are regulated by a state, MSQHPs will be licensed by states, but regulated by OPM. For example, OPM has the authority to certify, recertify, and decertify MSQHPs for participation in an exchange. If OPM certifies an MSQHP, the MSQHP is deemed certified to participate in every state's exchange.[98]

Child-Only Qualified Health Plans

ACA requires an issuer that offers a QHP through an exchange to also offer that plan as a "child-only plan."[99] Child-only plans will provide QHP coverage for individuals who are less than 21 years of age. The final regulation on exchanges stated that a child-only plan must be provided at the same level of coverage (bronze, silver, gold, or platinum) as a qualified health plan, as specified in the law.[100]

Consumer Operated and Oriented Plans

ACA establishes the Consumer Operated and Oriented Plan (CO-OP) program, with an intent to "foster the creation of qualified nonprofit health insurance issuers to offer qualified health plans in the individual and small group markets in the states in which the issuers are licensed to offer such plans."[101]

ACA authorizes $3.4 billion for the program that the HHS Secretary will use to finance start-up and solvency loans to non-profit organizations applying to become qualified issuers.[102]

Health plans offered by a CO-OP loan recipient may be deemed certified as a CO-OP QHP; if a plan is deemed a CO-OP QHP, then an exchange must recognize the plan as eligible to participate in an exchange. CO-OP QHPs are eligible to participate in an exchange for two years and may be recertified every two years after that for up to 10 years following the life of any loan awarded.

To be deemed certified, a CO-OP QHP must comply with the following: standards for certifying QHPs; all state-specific standards established by an exchange for QHPs operating in that state (except where those standards operate to exclude loan recipients due to being new issuers or based on characteristics that are inherent to being a CO-OP); and the standards of the CO-OP program as set forth in the law and the final rule relating to the CO-OP program.[103] CMS, or an entity designated by CMS, has the authority to deem CO-OP QHPs as certified to participate in an exchange.

CO-OP loan recipients must offer a CO-OP QHP at the silver and gold levels in every individual market exchange that serves the geographic regions in which the CO-OP loan recipient is licensed and intends to provide health care coverage.

If offering at least one plan in the small group market, CO-OP loan recipients must offer a CO-OP QHP at both the silver and gold levels in each SHOP that serves the geographic regions in which the entity is offering coverage.

This indicates that CO-OP QHPs will be offered in at least the individual market in every exchange that shares a geographic region with a CO-OP loan recipient.[104] Individuals who enroll in CO-OP QHPs offered through the individual market are eligible for premium tax credits and cost-sharing subsidies.

Catastrophic Plan

Issuers may offer catastrophic plans in the exchanges,[105] which will have actuarial values less than what is required to meet any of the levels of plan generosity for qualified health plans (described above).

These plans are expected to have lower premiums, because they will have less generous coverage and higher cost-sharing. Catastrophic plans must

- be available only to individuals under 30 years of age, or individuals exempt from the individual mandate,[106] because they do not have access to affordable coverage or experienced a hardship;
- include coverage for "essential health benefits";
- include coverage for at least three primary care visits;
- have a deductible equal to existing cost-sharing limits specified in the tax code, relating to certain high deductible health plans[107] (the deductible will not apply to "preventive health services"[108]); and
- be offered only through the individual health insurance market.

Stand-Alone Dental Benefits

ACA allows issuers to offer stand-alone dental benefits through the exchanges, as long as such benefits include pediatric oral services (as specified under the essential health benefits provision).[109]

The final exchange regulation clarifies that stand-alone dental benefits may be offered in a plan separate from a qualified health plan, or in conjunction with a QHP, as specified in the law. Exchanges may not limit the offer of stand-alone dental benefits to only one of these two options. In other words, issuers have sole discretion regarding (1) whether they will offer stand-alone dental benefits, and (2) the form in which those benefits will be provided (separate from or in conjunction with a QHP).

Cost Assistance

To make exchange coverage more affordable, certain individuals will receive premium assistance in the form of federal tax credits.[110] (As specified in the law, the Treasury Department will send monthly payments to the insurance company which issues the health plan in which a credit recipient is enrolled, to cover all or part of that person's monthly premium).[111] Moreover, some recipients of premium credits may also receive subsidies towards cost-sharing expenses.[112]

Exchanges have some responsibilities, as outlined below, in regard to determining an individual's eligibility for cost assistance and calculating the amount of cost assistance provided.

Premium Tax Credits

New federal tax credits were authorized in ACA to help low-middle income individuals pay for exchange coverage, beginning in 2014. The premium credit will be an advanceable, refundable tax credit, meaning tax filers need not wait until the end of the tax year in order to benefit from the credit (advance payments will actually go directly to the issuer),[113] and may claim the full credit amount even if they have little or no federal income tax liability.

To be eligible for a premium credit in an exchange, an individual must

- have household income[114] between 100% and 400% of the federal poverty level, with exceptions;[115]
- *not* be eligible for Medicaid or Medicare or other types of "minimum essential coverage"[116] (other than through the individual health insurance market);
- be enrolled in an exchange plan; and
- be part of a tax-filing unit.

The amount of the tax credit will vary from person to person: it depends on the household income of the tax filer (and dependents), the premium for the exchange plan in which the tax filer (and dependents) is (are) enrolled, and other factors. In certain instances, the credit amount may cover the entire premium and the tax filer pays nothing towards the premium. In other instances, the tax filer may be required to pay part (or all) of the premium.[117]

Exchanges are responsible for either determining an individual's eligibility for advance payment of premium credits or implementing a determination made by HHS.[118] If an exchange makes the determination, then the exchange is also responsible for calculating the amount of the credit in accordance with section 36B of the Internal Revenue Code.

Cost-Sharing Subsidies

Certain individuals who are eligible for premium credits in the exchanges will also be eligible for subsidies towards service-related cost-sharing. (According to guidance issued by HHS, the federal government will provide monthly payments to the issuer of the health plan in which the subsidy recipient is enrolled, to reduce the amount of cost-sharing that individual would be responsible for when s/he uses health services.[119]) An individual who qualifies for the premium credit *and* is enrolled in a silver plan[120] through an exchange, will also be eligible for a cost-sharing subsidy. As discussed above, total cost-sharing in exchange plans will be limited according to amounts specified in the federal tax code.[121] Given that most exchange plans will already be required to meet such limits, the cost-sharing subsidies will further reduce the total amount those individuals who qualify for the subsidies will pay for using health services.[122]

Exchanges are required to either determine an individual's eligibility for cost-sharing subsidies or implement a determination made by HHS.[123] To do this, an exchange is expected to collect and verify the information necessary to make the determination and share that information with HHS.

Interaction with Other ACA Provisions

Individual Mandate

Beginning in 2014, most individuals are required to have health insurance or potentially pay a penalty for noncompliance.[124] Generally, individuals will be required to maintain "minimum essential coverage" for themselves and their dependents.[125]

Nearly all plans offered through exchanges qualify as minimum essential coverage. As follows, most individuals who have coverage through an exchange will meet the requirements of the individual mandate. Other coverage, such as employer-sponsored insurance and Medicaid, is also considered minimum essential coverage for the purpose of the individual mandate, so an individual does not have to enroll in an exchange plan to meet the requirements of the mandate.

Certain individuals will be exempt from the individual mandate. For example, some individuals will qualify for an exemption based on the affordability of coverage while others will qualify because of their religious beliefs. In screening applicants for eligibility for QHPs and IAPs, exchanges are required to determine whether an individual is exempt from the mandate and issue certificates of exemption accordingly.[126]

Employer Requirements

While employers are not required to offer health benefits to their employees, certain large employers may be subject to penalties whether or not they offer health insurance. Large employers who do *not* offer health insurance may be subject to penalties if any of their *full-time* workers enroll in exchange plans and receive premium credits. While most employers who do offer health benefits will meet the law's requirements, some also may be required to pay a penalty if any of their full-time workers receive a premium credit.[127]

In the latter scenario, one way that workers with an employer offer of health benefits may be eligible for premium credits is if the employer plan does not provide minimum value; that is, has an actuarial value that is less than 60%.[128]

So while employers are not required to offer coverage through the exchanges, certain large employers may be subject to a penalty if they offer coverage with an actuarial value lower than a bronze-level plan and one of their full-time workers enrolls in an exchange and receives a premium credit.

Exchanges are responsible for notifying an employer if an employee has been found eligible for advance payment of premium credits or cost-sharing subsidies. The exchange must identify the employee, indicate the employee's eligibility, explain that the employer may be subject to penalty, and notify the employer of the right to appeal the determination.

Reforms to Private Health Insurance Markets

ACA includes a number of private market reforms that impose requirements on health insurance carriers and others. Such reforms relate to the offer, issuance, generosity, and pricing of health plans, among other requirements. For example, ACA requires most health plans to extend dependent coverage to children under age 26, with exception.[129] Given that health insurance carriers will be offering plans through the exchanges, ACA's private market reforms will apply to exchange plans.[130]

As discussed under the "Plan Management Responsibilities" section of this report, one of the responsibilities of exchanges will be to certify that plans meet the criteria for a qualified health plan, and, therefore, may be offered through an exchange.

While the certification process will consider plan marketing requirements, provider network adequacy, and other features, as specified in the law, the market reforms are requirements imposed generally on insurance companies. Since states remain the primary regulators of health insurance, even post-ACA enactment, states would enforce ACA insurance requirements.

Medicaid

While Medicaid is generally beyond the scope of this report, ACA's Medicaid and exchange provisions were originally designed to work in tandem with each other to provide a continuous source of subsidized coverage for low- to middle-income individuals and families, beginning in 2014. As previously discussed, exchanges are responsible for facilitating enrollment in Medicaid.

As *originally* enacted, ACA required states to expand Medicaid to certain individuals who are under age 65 with income up to 133%[131] of the federal poverty level (FPL), beginning in 2014. This reform not only expanded eligibility to a group that generally is not eligible for Medicaid (low-income childless adults), but also raised Medicaid's mandatory income eligibility level for certain existing groups to 133% of the FPL. States were required to do this mandatory expansion as a condition of receipt of Medicaid federal financial participation. Given that premium credits would be available through all state exchanges at the same time as this Medicaid expansion, the law envisioned that all individuals with income up to 400% FPL would have access to subsidized coverage, regardless of their state of residency.

On June 28, 2012, the United States Supreme Court issued its decision in *National Federation of Independent Business v. Sebelius*. The Court held that the federal government cannot terminate current Medicaid program federal matching funds if a state refuses to expand its Medicaid program to include non-elderly, non-pregnant adults under 133% of the federal poverty level. If a state accepts the new ACA Medicaid expansion funds, it must abide by the new expansion coverage rules, but, based on the Court's opinion, it appears that a state can refuse to participate in the expansion without losing any of its current federal Medicaid matching funds. All other provisions of ACA, including the entire Health Care and Education Reconciliation Act (HCERA, P.L. 111-152), remain intact. Given that some states may choose not to expand Medicaid, there is a possibility that some individuals will not have access to either Medicaid or the premium tax credits.

Regardless of whether or not a state expands its Medicaid program, the rules for coordination and facilitating enrollment between exchange plans and Medicaid will still apply.

For example, an individual exchange may decide to determine eligibility for Medicaid.[132] If a person who has applied for exchange coverage is determined eligible for Medicaid, the individual exchange must enroll the person in Medicaid and share the person's information with the state Medicaid agency.

Appendix A. Selected Exchange Implementation Dates

Table A-1. Selected Upcoming Exchange Implementation Dates

Date	Requirement
3rd Quarter, CY2012	States must specify a benchmark plan to serve as the reference plan for the essential health benefits (EHB) for coverage years 2014 and 2015.[a]
November 16, 2012	States seeking to administer all or part of their exchanges must submit a complete exchange blueprint no later than this date to be considered for exchange approval by January 1, 2013.
January 1, 2013	Each exchange must be approved to operate by HHS no later than this date in order to be operational on January 1, 2014.
October 1, 2013	Open enrollment must begin for coverage offered through an exchange for the 2014 coverage year.
January 1, 2014	Exchanges must be established and offer coverage in every state.

Source: Table prepared by CRS based on information collected from (1) ACA (P.L. 111-148, as amended); (2) *77 Federal Register* 18310; and (3) *Draft Blueprint for Approval of Affordable State-based and State Partnership Insurance Exchanges*, at http://cciio.cms.gov/resources/files/Exchangeblueprint05162012.pdf.

[a] This information was included in the Essential Health Benefits Bulletin released by HHS in December 2011. The bulletin provides information about the regulatory approach HHS intends to propose to define EHB. To date, HHS has not published regulations relating to EHB. The EHB Bulletin is available at http://cciio.cms.gov/resources/files/Files2/12162011/essential_health_benefits_bulletin.pdf.

Appendix B. Risk Mitigation Programs under ACA

Table B-1. Description of Reinsurance, Risk Corridors, and Risk-Adjustment Provisions of ACA

	Reinsurance	Risk Corridors	Risk- Adjustment
Description	Reinsurance typically is thought of as insurance for insurers. When issuing policies, an insurer faces the risk that the premiums it collects will not be sufficient to cover its expenses and generate profit. Reinsurance shifts the risk of covering high expenses from the primary insurer to a reinsurer. ACA requires all health insurance issuers and third-party administrators of group health plans to contribute to a reinsurance program administered by a nonprofit reinsurance entity.	Risk corridors refer to a mechanism that adjusts payments to health plans according to a formula based on each plan's actual, allowed expenses in relation to a target amount. If a plan's expenses exceed a certain percentage above the target, the plan's payment is increased. Likewise, if a plan's expenses exceed a certain percentage below the target, the plan's payment is decreased. Under ACA, a QHP issuer whose gains are greater than 3% of the issuer's "projections" must remit charges to HHS, while HHS must make payments to a QHP issuer that experiences losses that are greater than 3% of the issuer's "projections."	Risk adjustment refers to a mechanism that adjusts payments to health plans to take into account the risk that each plan is bearing based on its enrollee population. Plans with enrollment of less than average risk will pay an assessment to the state. States will provide payments to plans with higher than average risk.
Objective	Provide funding to plans that enroll highest cost individuals	Limit issuer loss (and gains)	Transfer funds from lowest risk plans to highest risk plans
Goal	Offset high-cost outliers	Protect against inaccurate rate setting	Protect against adverse selection
Who Participates	Non-grandfathered individual market plans (inside and outside of exchange) are eligible for payments	Qualified Health Plans (QHPs) in the individual and small group markets (inside and outside of exchange)	Non-grandfathered individual and small group market plans (inside and outside the exchange, excluding self-insured plans)
Time Frame	Three years (2014-2016)	Three years (2014-2016)	Permanent; begins after end of benefit year 2014

Source: CRS analysis of ACA.

End Notes

[1] "Utah Health Exchange," http://www.exchange.utah.gov/about-the-exchange.

[2] "Health Connector," https://www.mahealthconnector.org/portal/site/connector.

[3] The private health insurance market is made up of three segments—the large group, small group and nongroup (individual) markets. The nongroup market refers to insurance policies offered to individuals and families buying insurance on their own. Group insurance refers to health plans offered through a plan sponsor, typically an employer.

[4] Before 2016, states will have the option to define "small employers" either as those with 100 or fewer employees or 50 or fewer employees. Beginning in 2016, small employers will be defined as those with 100 or fewer employees. Beginning in 2017, states may allow large employers to obtain coverage through an exchange (but will not be required to do so).

[5] With the exception of stand-alone dental plans that are allowed to be offered in the exchanges.

[6] For additional information about ACA's private market reforms, see CRS Report R42069, *Private Health Insurance* Market Reforms in the Patient Protection and Affordable Care Act (ACA), by Annie L. Mach and Bernadette Fernandez.

[7] As discussed in the "Plan Management Responsibilities" section of this report, a plan has to meet certain statutory requirements to be certified as a QHP. Certain plans offered through exchanges (e.g., stand-alone dental plans) do not necessarily meet all of the criteria to be certified as a QHP; however, the plans are required to meet some criteria and are considered QHPs for the purpose of how the exchange interacts with the plan. For example, while a stand-alone dental plan cannot meet criteria related to benefits to qualify as a QHP (because the plan only offers dental benefits), a stand-alone dental plan is still required to meet the QHP standard to annually provide benefit and rate information to the exchange.

[8] §1312(d)(3)(B) of ACA.

[9] §1312(d)(1) of ACA.

[10] §§ 1311(b) and 1321(c) of ACA.

[11] 77 *Federal Register* 18310, March 27, 2012.

[12] §1311(b) of ACA. Guidance released May 16, 2012 provides more information about the approval process for exchanges. For more information, see http://cciio.cms.gov/resources/files/Exchangeblueprint05162012.pdf.

[13] §1321(c) of ACA.

[14] 77 *Federal Register* 18310, March 27, 2012. The law also requires that the HHS Secretary creates a process whereby states that were operating exchanges before January 1, 2010 can receive assistance from federal agencies to bring their exchanges into compliance with the requirements under ACA (§1322(e) of ACA).

[15] Selected exchange implementation dates are shown in **Table A-1**. It should be noted that the final rule on exchange establishment (77 *Federal Register* 18310, March 27, 2012) provides for ways in which states can change the type of exchange established in the state. For example, if a state chooses not to establish an exchange for 2014, it still may elect to do so in the future.

[16] For a comprehensive discussion of the premium tax credits, see CRS Report R41137, Health Insurance Premium Credits in the Patient Protection and Affordable Care Act (ACA), by Bernadette Fernandez and Thomas Gabe.

[17] 77 *Federal Register* 18310, March 27, 2012.

[18] In responding to requests for clarification regarding what would be considered "governmental," HHS has said that it will not offer further clarification of "governmental" in deference to existing state classifications. HHS has not commented on the definition of a non-profit established by a state.

[19] §1311(f)(1) of ACA. Each state participating in the regional exchange must permit the operation of the regional exchange, and the HHS Secretary has to approve the regional exchange before it can begin operation.

[20] §1311(f)(2) of ACA. The area served by a subsidiary exchange must be at least as large as a rating area approved by the HHS Secretary for purposes described in §2701 of the Public Health Service Act (PHSA).

[21] §1311(b)(2) of ACA.

[22] 77 *Federal Register* 18310, March 27, 2012.

[23] §1311(f)(3) of ACA and 77 *Federal Register* 18310, March 27, 2012. If an exchange contracts out any function of the exchange, the exchange is responsible for ensuring that the contracted entity meets all federal requirements related to the function.

[24] 77 *Federal Register* 18310, March 27, 2012.

[25] Ibid.

[26] §1321(c) of ACA.

[27] The partnership model is discussed in an HHS fact sheet published September 19, 2011, available at http://www.healthcare.gov/news/factsheets/2011/09/exchanges09192011a.html. The partnership model and the federally-facilitated exchange model are both discussed in the final rule on establishment of exchanges (77 *Federal Register* 18310, March 27, 2012). Finally, more information is provided about federally-facilitated exchanges, including partnerships, in guidance released May 16, 2012, available at http://cciio.cms.gov/resources/files/FFE_Guidance_FINAL_VERSION_051612.pdf.

[28] 77 *Federal Register* 18310, March 27, 2012.

[29] Center for Consumer Information and Insurance Oversight, *General Guidance on Federally-facilitated Exchanges*, May 16, 2012, http://cciio.cms.gov/resources/files/FFE_Guidance_FINAL_VERSION_051612.pdf.

[30] The framework for this section is adapted from a report co-authored by Deborah Bachrach and Patricia Boozang, titled, "Federally-Facilitated Exchanges and the Continuum of State Options," available at http://www.nasi.org/ research/2011/federally-facilitated-exchanges-continuum-state-options.

[31] ACA requires states to establish procedures that ensure that the state's Medicaid and CHIP agencies also establish a streamlined eligibility and enrollment process that coordinates with the exchange's process.

[32] For more information about QHPs offered through an exchange, see the "Qualified Health Plans" section of this report.

[33] The term and definition of "insurance affordability programs" is adopted from a definition in the final rule on exchange establishment (77 *Federal Register* 18310, March 27, 2012).

[34] §1331 of ACA requires the HHS Secretary to create a basic health program (BHP), which is a health insurance program for low-income individuals who are not eligible for Medicaid, and is offered in lieu of eligible individuals obtaining coverage through an exchange. States have the option to implement the BHP, and therefore, exchanges will interact with BHPs in only those states that choose to implement a BHP.

[35] 77 *Federal Register* 18310, March 27, 2012.

[36] Ibid.

[37] These provisions were included as "interim final" rather than in the final rule on exchange establishment (77 *Federal Register* 18310, March 27, 2012), and comments were accepted on both provisions through May 11, 2012. The preamble of the final rule indicates that further guidance on these provisions is forthcoming.

[38] The eligibility criteria for advance payment of premium tax credits and cost-sharing subsidies are the same regardless of whether an individual exchange makes the determination or HHS makes the determination.

[39] On June 28, 2012, the United States Supreme Court issued its decision in *National Federation of Independent Business v. Sebelius*. The Court held that the federal government cannot terminate current Medicaid program federal matching funds if a state refuses to expand its Medicaid program to include non-elderly, non-pregnant adults under 133% of the federal poverty level. If a state accepts the new ACA Medicaid expansion funds, it must abide by the new expansion coverage rules, but, based on the Court's opinion, it appears that a state

can refuse to participate in the expansion without losing any of its current federal Medicaid matching funds. This decision did not affect the ACA requirement that modified adjusted gross income (MAGI) would be the new income test for most of Medicaid's covered populations beginning in 2014. For a legal analysis of the Court's decision on Medicaid, see CRS General Distribution Memorandum, *Selected Issues Related to the Effect of NFIB v. Sebelius on the Medicaid Expansion Requirements in Section 2001 of the Affordable Care Act*, by Kathleen S. Swendiman and Evelyne P. Baumrucker. For a comprehensive discussion about MAGI and ACA, see CRS Report R41997, *Definition of Income in ACA for Certain Medicaid Provisions and Premium Credits*, coordinated by Janemarie Mulvey.

[40] Before 2016, states will have the option to define "small employers" either as those with 100 or fewer employees or 50 or fewer employees. Beginning in 2016, small employers will be defined as those with 100 or fewer employees.

[41] Beginning in 2017, a state may also allow an issuer of coverage in the large group market to offer QHPs in the large group market through an exchange. If that is the case, then a qualified employer would also include an employer in the large group market.

[42] 77 *Federal Register* 18310, March 27, 2012.

[43] Ibid. If a state merges its individual and small group risk pools, as is allowed under §1312(c)(3) of ACA, then the SHOP may permit an employee to enroll in any QHP (including one offered in the individual market), as long as the QHP meets certain requirements for small group market plans.

[44] §1311(d)(4)(A) of ACA.

[45] Except that, according to §1311(e)(1)(B) of ACA, the exchange may not exclude a plan because it is a fee-for-service plan, through the imposition of price controls, or on the basis that the plan provides treatments necessary to prevent patients' deaths in circumstances the exchange determines are inappropriate or too costly.

[46] In the final regulation on entities for the accreditation of exchange plans, HHS stated that the National Committee for Quality Assurance and URAC (formerly known as the Utilization Review Accreditation Commission) would serve as accrediting entities during the first phase of the accrediting process. HHS will consider other accrediting bodies and individual states at a later time. 77 *Federal Register* 42662, July 20, 2012.

[47] §1311(c)(1) of ACA and 77 *Federal Register* 18310, March 27, 2012.

[48] §1311(e)(2) of ACA.

[49] §1311(d)(4) of ACA. In the final rule on the establishment of exchanges (77 *Federal Register* 18310, March 27, 2012) it is indicated that the rating system will be addressed in future rulemaking.

[50] HHS more specifically describes the consumer assistance functions of federally-facilitated exchanges, including partnerships, in guidance available at http://cciio.cms.gov/resources/files/FFE_Guidance_FINAL_VERSION_051612.pdf.

[51] The standard format an exchange is expected to use to present QHPs is required to include the uniform outline of coverage as established under §2715 of the PHSA (§1001 of ACA). For more information about the uniform outline of coverage, see CRS Report R42069, *Private Health Insurance Market Reforms in the Patient Protection and Affordable Care Act (ACA)*, by Annie L. Mach and Bernadette Fernandez.

[52] The final rule on exchange establishment (77 *Federal Register* 18310, March 27, 2012) does not specify the content or quantity of these outreach and education activities, but it does require that the activities must be accessible to all audiences, including to individuals with disabilities and those with limited English proficiency.

[53] §1311(i) of ACA and 77 *Federal Register* 18310, March 27, 2012.

[54] §1311(c)(4) of ACA. The survey is only for those QHPs that had more than 500 enrollees in the previous year. To date, HHS has not released any information about this survey.

[55] §1311(d)(6) of ACA.

[56] §1311(d)(7) of ACA.

[57] 77 *Federal Register* 18310, March 27, 2012.

[58] Ibid.

[59] §1311(d)(5) of ACA.

[60] 77 Federal Register 18310, March 27, 2012.

[61] §1313 of ACA.

[62] These criteria are included in the final rule related to the establishment of exchanges (77 *Federal Register* 18310, arch 27, 2012).

[63] For an overview of the rulemaking authority given to federal agencies under ACA, see CRS Report R42431, *Upcoming Rules Pursuant to the Patient Protection and Affordable Care Act: Fall 2011 Unified Agenda*, by Maeve P. Carey and Michelle D. Christensen.

[64] §1321(a)(1) of ACA.

[65] §1411(c) of ACA.

[66] §1311 of ACA.

[67] The CRS Congressional Distribution (CD) memorandum, "Patient Protection and Affordable Care Act: Health Insurance Exchange Planning and Establishment Grants" by C. Stephen Redhead and Annie L. Mach, includes a table that shows the federal grants (discussed in this section) that have been awarded to each state and the District of Columbia. The memorandum is available upon request from the memorandum's authors.

[68] §1311(a) of ACA. Some contend that the law does not contain explicit appropriation authority for the operation of federally-facilitated exchanges, as §1311 only says that the Secretary may award planning and establishment grants to states. However, in regard to the federally-facilitated exchange, the law does say that, "...the Secretary shall (directly or through agreement with a not-for-profit entity) establish and operate such exchange within the state and the Secretary shall take such actions as are necessary to implement such other requirements" (§1321(c)(1)(B)).

[69] All exchanges are expected to be self-sustaining by January 1, 2015. In guidance, however, HHS clarified that planning and establishment grants awarded through December 31, 2014 may be used for approved establishment activities after that date. For more information, see http://cciio.cms.gov/resources/files/Files2/11282011/exchange_q_and_a.pdf.pdf.

[70] Alaska is the only state that did not apply for a planning grant. Three states, Florida, Louisiana, and New Hampshire, have stated that they plan to return some or all of their planning grant funds. For more information about which states have received grants, see http://www.healthcare.gov/news/factsheets/2011/05/exchanges05232011a.html.

[71] The 34 states that have received a level one grant so far are: AL, AZ, AR, CA, CO, CT, DE, HI, ID, IL, IN, IA, KY, ME, MD, MA, MI, MN, MS, MO, NE, NV, NJ, NM, NY, NC, OR, PA, RI, SD, TN, VT, WA, and WV. The states that have received level two grants, to date, are Rhode Island and Washington.

[72] Center for Consumer Information and Insurance Oversight, "Affordable Insurance Exchanges: Update and Upcoming Implementation Forums," press release, May 16, 2012, http://cciio.cms.gov/resources/factsheets/ affordable_insurance_exchanges.html.

[73] §1561 of ACA: §3021 of PHSA.

[74] The seven grantees are Kansas, Maryland, New York, Oklahoma, Oregon, Wisconsin, and a multi-state consortium led by the University of Massachusetts Medical School (which includes Connecticut, Maine, Massachusetts, Rhode Island, and Vermont). Three states, Kansas, Oklahoma, and Wisconsin, have since stated their intention to return some or all of the grant. For more information, see http://www.cbpp.org/files/CBPP-Analysis-on-the-Status-of-State-Exchange-Implementation.pdf.

[75] HealthCare.gov, "States Leading the Way on Implementation: HHS Awards "Early Innovator" Grants to Seven States," press release, February 16, 2011, http://www.healthcare.gov/news/factsheets/2011/02/exchanges02162011a.html.

[76] Center for Consumer Information and Insurance Oversight, "Affordable Insurance Exchanges: Update and Upcoming Implementation Forums," press release, May 16, 2012, http://cciio.cms.gov/resources/factsheets/affordable_insurance_exchanges.html.

[77] §1302(a)-(d) of ACA.

[78] This applies to all exchange enrollees whose insurance is affected by additional state benefit mandates, not just those exchange enrollees eligible for premium tax credits and cost-sharing subsidies. §1311(d)(3)(B) of ACA.

[79] See "Selected Medical Benefits: A Report from the Department of Labor to the Department of Health and Human Services," Department of Labor, April 15, 2011, http://www.bls.gov/ncs/ebs/sp/selmedbensreport.pdf.

[80] "Essential Health Benefits Bulletin," Center for Consumer Information and Insurance Oversight, December 16, 2011, p.8, http://cciio.cms.gov/resources/files/Files2/12162011/essential_health_benefits_bulletin.pdf.

[81] In the final regulation on data collection to support essential health benefits standards, HHS stated that it will collect data from the insurance carriers that offer the three largest health plans (by enrollment) in the small group market within each state. The data collection is for purposes of identifying a potential "default benchmark plan" for each state. HHS intends to make publicly available the "information on the final state selections of benchmarks...as soon as possible." 77 *Federal Register* 42661, July 20, 2012.

[82] See "Essential Health Benefits: Comparing Benefits in Small Group Products and State and Federal Employee Plans," Office of the Assistant Secretary for Planning and Evaluation, December 2011, http://aspe.hhs.gov/health/reports/2011/MarketComparison/rb.shtml; "Essential Health Benefits: List of the Largest Three Small Group Products by State," Center for Consumer Information and Insurance Oversight, July 3, 2012, http://cciio.cms.gov/resources/files/largest-smgroup-products-7-2-2012.pdf.PDF; and "Frequently Asked Questions on Essential Health Benefits Bulletin," Centers for Medicare and Medicaid Services, February 17, 2012, http://cciio.cms.gov/resources/files/Files2/02172012/ ehb-faq-508.pdf.

[83] While this provision specifically applies these deductible limits to small group health plans, § 1201 of ACA: new PHSA § 2707 also applies these limits to "group health plans" broadly.

[84] The cost-sharing limits that are part of the essential health benefits package mirror the limits applicable to high-deductible health plans (HDHPs) that qualify to be paired with health savings accounts (HSAs). For 2012, the cost-sharing limits for HSA-qualified HDHPs are $6,050 for single coverage, and $12,100 for family coverage. Given that the existing limits are updated annually and ACA cost-sharing requirements become effective in 2014, the cost-sharing limits in 2014 will likely be different than the 2012 levels.

[85] While actuarial value (AV) is a useful measure, it is only one component that addresses the value of any given benefit package. AV, by itself, does not address other important features of coverage, such as total (dollar) value, network adequacy, and premiums.

[86] While actuarial value is calculated based on costs for an entire population, it does not mean that every person enrolled in the same plan will have the same expenses, because in any given group some people use relatively little care while others use a great deal. Given that actuarial value reflects cost-sharing, such a measure may be useful to consumers when comparing different health plans.

[87] "Critical Issues in Health Reform: Actuarial Equivalence," American Academy of Actuaries, May 2009, p. 4, available online at http://www.actuary.org/pdf/health/equivalence_may09.pdf.

[88] "Actuarial Value and Cost-Sharing Reductions Bulletin," Center for Consumer Information and Insurance Oversight, February 24, 2012, http://cciio.cms.gov/resources/files/Files2/02242012/Av-csr-bulletin.pdf, p. 5.

[89] For more information about these plan types, see the "Multi-state Qualified Health Plans" and the "Consumer Operated and Oriented Plans" sections of this report.

[90] For more information about these plan types, see the "Child-Only Qualified Health Plans" and the "Catastrophic Plan" sections of this report.

[91] Plans that are offered both inside and outside of exchanges must charge the same premium. In addition, ACA allows the types of health plans that are currently offered in the private

market to continue to be offered once the exchanges have been established, as long as those other plan types comply with applicable federal and state law.

[92] §1301 of ACA.

[93] §1311(c) of ACA.

[94] §1301(a)(1)(C)(iii) of ACA; and 77 *Federal Register* 18415, March 27, 2012.

[95] §1334 of ACA.

[96] §1334(a) of ACA.

[97] OPM administers FEHBP and, among other duties, is authorized to negotiate benefit and premium levels with health plans that participate in FEHBP. For more information about OPM's role in FEHBP, see CRS Report RS21974, *Federal Employees Health Benefits Program: Available Health Insurance Options*, by Annie L. Mach.

[98] 77 *Federal Register* 18310, March 27, 2012. To date, OPM has not yet promulgated regulations related to MSQHPs.

[99] §1302(f) of ACA.

[100] 77 *Federal Register*, 18469, March 27, 2012.

[101] §1322(a)(2) of ACA.

[102] ACA appropriated $6 billion to the CO-OP program. The Department of Defense and Full-Year Continuing Appropriations Act, 2011 (P.L. 112-10) canceled $2.2 billion of the appropriations, and the Consolidated Appropriations Act, 2012 (P.L. 112-74) canceled an additional $400 million of the appropriations for the CO-OP program.

[103] §1322 of ACA and 76 *Federal Register* 77392, December 13, 2011.

[104] According to the final rule on CO-OPs (76 *Federal Register* 77392, December 13, 2011), only two-thirds of plans offered by CO-OP loan recipients must be CO-OP QHPs offered in the individual and small group markets, indicating that CO-OP loan recipients may offer health plans that will not necessarily be available in the individual and small group markets, whether inside or outside an exchange (i.e., Medicare managed care plans).

[105] § 1302(e) of ACA.

[106] Beginning in 2014, ACA requires individuals to maintain health insurance, with some exceptions. For additional information about this provision, see CRS Report R41331, *Individual Mandate and Related Information Requirements under ACA*, by Janemarie Mulvey and Hinda Chaikind.

[107] The deductible for exchange catastrophic plans mirror the cost-sharing limits applicable to high-deductible health plans (HDHPs) that qualify to be paired with health savings accounts (HSAs). For 2012, the cost-sharing limits for HSA-qualified HDHPs are $6,050 for single coverage, and $12,100 for family coverage. Given that the existing limits are updated annually and the exchanges become operational in 2014, the deductible for exchange catastrophic plans in 2014 will likely be different than the 2012 HDHP/HSA limits.

[108] § 1001 of ACA; Section 2713 of the Public Health Service Act.

[109] §1311(d)(2)(B)(ii) of ACA.

[110] §1401 of ACA.

[111] While a premium credit recipient could choose to wait until the end of the tax year to claim the credit, as part of filing federal income taxes, the most likely scenario is for that individual to choose to receive the tax credit in the form of advanced payments, to coincide with the monthly payment of insurance premiums.

[112] §1402 of ACA.

[113] §1412(a)(3) of ACA.

[114] Household income is measured according to the current tax definition for "modified adjusted gross income" (MAGI). For a comprehensive discussion about MAGI and ACA, see CRS Report R41997, *Definition of Income in ACA for Certain Medicaid Provisions and Premium Credits*, coordinated by Janemarie Mulvey.

[115] An exception is made for lawfully present aliens with income below 100% of the FPL, who are ineligible for Medicaid for the first five years that they are lawfully present. These

taxpayers will be treated as though their income is exactly 100% of FPL for purposes of the premium credit.

[116] The definition of minimum essential coverage is broad. It includes Medicare Part A, Medicaid, the State Children's Health Insurance Program (CHIP), Tricare, the TRICARE for Life program, the veteran's health care program, the Peace Corps program, a government plan (local, state, federal) including the Federal Employees Health Benefits Program (FEHBP) and any plan established by an Indian tribal government, any plan offered in the individual, small group or large group market, a grandfathered health plan, and any other health benefits coverage, such as a state health benefits risk pool, as recognized by the HHS Secretary in coordination with the Treasury Secretary.

[117] For a comprehensive discussion of the premium tax credits, including illustrative examples of possible credit amounts, see CRS Report R41137, *Health Insurance Premium Credits in the Patient Protection and Affordable Care Act (ACA)*, by Bernadette Fernandez and Thomas Gabe.

[118] See the "Eligibility for Premium Tax Credits and Cost-Sharing Subsidies" section in this report for more information.

[119] This proposed approach for implementing the cost-sharing subsidies was discussed in a bulletin issued by HHS: "Actuarial Value and Cost-Sharing Reductions Bulletin," February 24, 2012, -http://cciio.cms.gov/resources/files/Files2/02242012/Av-csr-bulletin.pdf.

[120] See previous discussion of precious metal designations for exchange plans under the section "Levels of Plan Generosity" in this report.

[121] The cost-sharing limits that are part of the essential health benefits package mirror the limits applicable to high-deductible health plans (HDHPs) that qualify to be paired with health savings accounts (HSAs). For 2012, the cost-sharing limits for HSA-qualified HDHPs are $6,050 for single coverage, and $12,100 for family coverage. Given that the existing limits are updated annually and ACA cost-sharing requirements become effective in 2014, the cost-sharing limits in 2014 will likely be different than the 2012 levels.

[122] For additional information about the cost-sharing subsidies, including illustrative examples, see CRS Report R41137, *Health Insurance Premium Credits in the Patient Protection and Affordable Care Act (ACA)*, by Bernadette Fernandez and Thomas Gabe.

[123] See the "Eligibility for Premium Tax Credits and Cost-Sharing Subsidies" section in this report for more information.

[124] The constitutionality of the individual mandate has been the centerpiece of numerous legal challenges to ACA. In March of 2012, the United States Supreme Court heard arguments related to the constitutionality question, along with other legal issues. On June 28, 2012, the Court issued its decision in *National Federation of Independent Business v. Sebelius*, finding that the individual mandate in § 5000A of the Internal Revenue Code (as added by § 1501 of the Patient Protection and Affordable Care Act (ACA)), is a constitutional exercise of Congress's authority to levy taxes. For additional discussion about the Court's decision, the individual mandate, and other ACA issues, see the CRS Legal Sidebar posts under "Health and Medicine," http://www.crs.gov/analysis/legalsidebar/pages/default.aspx?source=legalSidebar.

[125] For a list of the types of coverage that qualify as "minimum essential coverage" and additional information about the individual mandate see CRS Report R41331, *Individual Mandate and Related Information Requirements under ACA*, by Janemarie Mulvey and Hinda Chaikind.

[126] In the final rule on exchange establishment (77 *Federal Register* 18310, March 27, 2012), HHS indicated that in future rulemaking it will address the process exchanges will use to provide certificates of exemption.

[127] For additional information about employer requirements under ACA, see CRS Report R41159, *Summary of Potential Employer Penalties Under the Patient Protection and Affordable Care Act (PPACA)*, by Janemarie Mulvey.

[128] §1401(a) of ACA; adding a new §36B(c)(2)(C) to the Internal Revenue Code.

[129] For additional information about ACA's private market reforms, see CRS Report R42069, *Private Health Insurance Market Reforms in the Patient Protection and Affordable Care Act (ACA)*, by Annie L. Mach and Bernadette.

[130] Note that ACA does not prohibit such carriers from offering coverage outside of exchanges – see §1312 (d)(1)(A) of ACA.

[131] In addition, there is a 5% income disregard, so that the limit is 138% of the FPL.

[132] For more information about an individual exchange's responsibilities relating to screening individuals for Medicaid, see the "Eligibility for Medicaid and CHIP" section in this report.

In: Health Insurance Exchanges ...
Editor: Edward J. Volpicelli
ISBN: 978-1-62417-367-7

Chapter 2

HEALTH INSURANCE PREMIUM CREDITS IN THE PATIENT PROTECTION AND AFFORDABLE CARE ACT (ACA)*

Bernadette Fernandez and Thomas Gabe

SUMMARY

New federal tax credits were authorized in the Patient Protection and Affordable Care Act (ACA, P.L. 111-148, as amended), to help certain individuals pay for health insurance coverage, beginning in 2014.

ACA requires "American Health Benefit Exchanges" to be established in every state by January 1, 2014, either by the state itself or by the Secretary of Health and Human Services (HHS). Exchanges will not be insurers, but will provide eligible individuals and small businesses with access to private health insurance plans. Generally, the plans offered through the exchanges will provide comprehensive coverage and meet all ACA market reforms, as applicable. One of the requirements that most exchange plans must meet is to provide a certain level of coverage generosity based on actuarial value. Each level of coverage generosity is designated according to a precious metal and corresponds to a specific actuarial value: Bronze (actuarial value of 60%), Silver (70%), Gold (80%), and Platinum (90%).

---

* This is an edited, reformatted and augmented version of the Congressional Research Service Publication, CRS Report for Congress R41137, dated June 13, 2012.

To make exchange coverage more affordable, certain individuals will receive premium assistance in the form of federal tax credits. The premium credit will be an advanceable, refundable tax credit, meaning taxpayers need not wait until the end of the tax year in order to benefit from the credit, and may claim the full credit amount even if they have little or no federal income tax liability. Although the premium credits will not be available until 2014, the illustrations provided in this report are based on current federal poverty levels, to reflect how the estimated premium credit amounts compare to current income levels.

Under ACA, the amount received in premium credits is based on income tax returns. These amounts are reconciled in the next year and can result in overpayment of premium credits if income increases, which must be repaid to the federal government. ACA limited the amount of required repayments. Since the enactment of ACA, these limits have been increased in order to raise revenues for other legislative initiatives (e.g., P.L. 111-309 and P.L. 112-9). Most recently, on June 7, 2012, the House passed H.R. 436, the Health Care Cost Reduction Act of 2012, which includes a measure that would remove all limits on repayment, making individuals fully liable for the full amount of any premium credit overpayment.

Relative affordability of health insurance premiums individuals and families might face within health insurance exchanges will likely vary from exchange to exchange based on a host of factors, including enrollees' age, the varying prices paid by plans for medical goods and services, the breadth of the provider network, the provisions regarding how out-of-network care is paid for (or not), and the use of tools by the plan to reduce health care utilization (e.g., prior authorization for certain tests). Examples provided in the Appendix of this report depict a range by which premiums might reasonably be expected to vary based on enrollees' age, and variation in medical costs across geographic areas, for purposes of illustration only. Actual premiums will likely vary among health insurance exchanges based on a wide range of factors other than those depicted in this report.

New federal tax credits were authorized in the Patient Protection and Affordable Care Act (ACA, P.L. 111-148, as amended), to help certain individuals pay for health insurance coverage, beginning in 2014. The tax credits will go towards the cost of purchasing coverage offered through health insurance exchanges—marketplaces offering comprehensive, private health plans.

This report describes who will be eligible for the premium credits,[1] and how the credit amounts will be calculated. It also highlights key issues raised by the Internal Revenue Service (IRS) in the notice of proposed rulemaking (NPRM) on the premium credits.[2] The Appendix provides analysis of the concept of "affordability" as applicable to the premium credits.

BACKGROUND

ACA[3] requires "American Health Benefit Exchanges" to be established in every state by January 1, 2014, either by the state itself or by the Secretary of Health and Human Services (HHS). Exchanges will not be insurers, but will provide eligible individuals and small businesses with access to private health insurance plans.[4]

Generally, the plans offered through the exchanges will provide comprehensive coverage and meet all ACA market reforms, as applicable. One of the requirements that most exchange plans must meet is to provide a certain level of coverage generosity based on actuarial value.[5] Each level of coverage generosity is designated according to a precious metal and corresponds to a specific actuarial value: Bronze (actuarial value of 60%), Silver (70%), Gold (80%), and Platinum (90%).

Certain individuals who enroll in exchange coverage will be eligible for premium assistance in the form of federal tax credits. The premium credit will be an advanceable, refundable tax credit, meaning taxpayers need not wait until the end of the tax year in order to benefit from the credit (advance payments will actually go directly to the insurer),[6] and may claim the full credit amount even if they have little or no federal income tax liability.

According to the Congressional Budget Office (CBO), 29 million individuals are projected to be enrolled in exchange coverage in 2019. Of those, 19 million are projected to receive premium credits[7] (see Figure 1).

As part of the ACA implementation process, the Treasury Department issued a notice of proposed rulemaking (NPRM), on the ACA premium credits in the Federal Register on August 17, 2011.[8] While the proposed rule confirmed certain eligibility and other requirements as specified in the statute, it also requested comments on various implementation issues, including flexibility with respect to the timing of eligibility (and ineligibility) for premium credits, employee and employer safe harbors, coverage of all family members in one or multiple plans, tax units with mid-year changes in family composition or filing status, and other issues. The NPRM also announced an opportunity for the public to present oral comments during a public hearing; it was held on November 17, 2011.

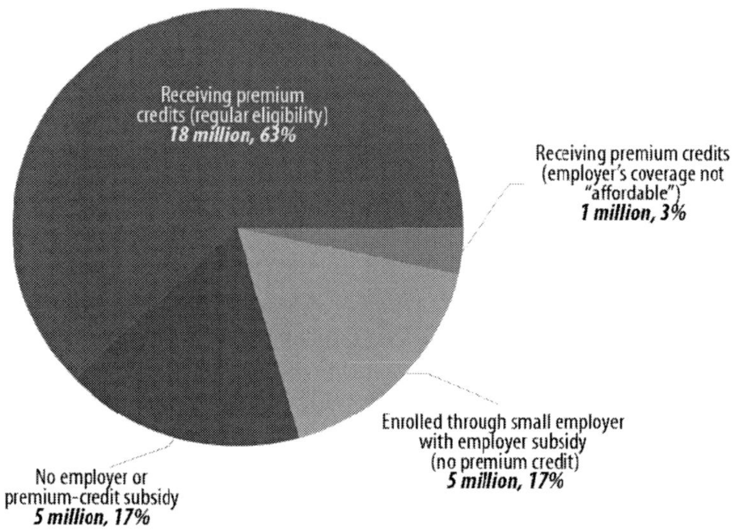

Source: CBO letter to Speaker Pelosi, ACA cost estimate, March 20, 2010, p. 9 and Table 4, http://cbo.gov/ ftpdocs/113xx/doc11379/AmendReconProp.pdf.

Note: Beginning in 2014, an employer's coverage is not "affordable" when the employee's contribution toward the employer's lowest-cost self-only premiums would exceed 9.5% of household income. Employees with an employer offer of coverage may also be eligible for premium credits if the employer plan does not provide minimum value (i.e., covers less than 60% of total allowed costs). However, the CBO projection of individuals for premium credits (besides meeting other eligibility criteria) because the employer plan would not provide minimum value was well under 1 million, and therefore not included in CBO published projections or in this figure.

Figure 1. CBO: Projected Exchange Enrollment, 2019.

INDIVIDUAL ELIGIBILITY FOR PREMIUM CREDITS

ACA specifies that premium credits will be available to "applicable taxpayers" in a "coverage month" beginning in 2014.

An *applicable taxpayer* is an individual who

- is part of a tax-filing unit,
- is enrolled in an exchange plan, and
- has household income between 100% and 400% of the federal poverty level (exception described below).

A *coverage month* refers to a month in which the applicable taxpayer paid for coverage offered through an exchange, not including any month in which the taxpayer was eligible for "minimum essential coverage" with exceptions (described below).

These eligibility criteria are discussed in greater detail below.

Part of a Tax-Filing Unit

Given that the premium assistance will be provided in the form of tax credits, they will be administered through individual tax returns (although advance payments will go directly to insurers).[9] The credits can only be obtained by qualifying individuals who file federal tax returns.

Couples married at the end of the taxable year will have to file joint returns to be eligible for the credit. The NPRM includes special rules relating to the calculation of credit amounts in response to changes in filing status (e.g., taxpayers who marry or divorce during tax year), and requests comments on related operational issues (e.g., flexibility in meeting the requirement for married couples to file jointly).

Enrolled in an Exchange Plan

Premium credits will only be available to individuals enrolled in a plan offered through an exchange.[10] Individuals may enroll in a plan through their state's exchange if they are (1) residing in a state in which an exchange was established; (2) not incarcerated, except individuals in custody pending the disposition of charges; and (3) lawful residents.

Only lawful residents may obtain exchange coverage. Undocumented aliens will be prohibited from obtaining coverage through an exchange, even if they could pay the entire premium without any subsidy.[11] Because ACA prohibits undocumented aliens from obtaining exchange coverage, they will not be eligible for premium credits.

The NPRM clarifies the potential credit eligibility for family members of individuals who themselves may not be eligible to enroll in an exchange due to incarceration or legal status (e.g., when there is a family of four and one of the family members is incarcerated).

Table 1. Income Levels at 400% FPL, 2011

Number of Persons in Family	48 Contiguous States and DC	Alaska	Hawaii
1	$43,560	$54,400	$50,160
2	$58,840	$73,520	$67,720
3	$74,120	$92,640	$85,280
4	$89,400	$111,760	$102,840
5	$104,680	$130,880	$120,400
6	$119,960	$150,000	$137,960
7	$135,240	$169,120	$155,520
8	$150,520	$188,240	$173,080

Source: CRS computation based on "Annual Update of the HHS Poverty Guidelines," 76 Federal Register 3637-3638, January 20, 2011, http://aspe.hhs.gov/poverty/11fedreg.pdf.

Notes: Under ACA, premium credits for eligible exchange coverage will not be available until 2014; the data in this table are for illustrative purposes only. The data are the income levels at which individuals would not be eligible for premium credits, if such credits were made available in 2011. "DC" is the District of Columbia. The Federal Poverty Guidelines are updated annually for inflation.

Household Income Is 100%-400% of Federal Poverty Level

To be eligible for premium credits, individuals must have "household income" within statutorily defined guidelines based on the federal poverty level (FPL).[12] For purposes of premium credit eligibility, household income is measured according to the current tax definition for "modified adjusted gross income" (MAGI).[13]

An individual whose MAGI is at or above 100% FPL up to 400% FPL may be eligible to receive premium credits,[14] beginning in 2014.[15]

For illustrative purposes only, Table 1 displays the income levels at 400% FPL, the amount at which individuals will no longer be eligible for any premium credit, if the credits were available in 2011.[16]

Not Eligible for "Minimum Essential Coverage"

To be eligible for a premium credit, an individual may *not* be *eligible* for "minimum essential coverage," with exceptions (described below). ACA broadly defines minimum essential coverage to include Medicare Part A,

Medicaid, the Children's Health Insurance Program (CHIP), Tricare, Tricare for Life, the veteran's health care program, the Peace Corps program, any government plan (local, state, federal) including the Federal Employees Health Benefits Program (FEHBP), any plan established by an Indian tribal government, any plan offered in the individual health insurance market, any employer-sponsored plan, any grandfathered health plan,[17] and any other coverage (such as a state high risk pool) recognized by the HHS Secretary.[18]

Exceptions to Minimum Essential Coverage Eligibility

ACA provides certain exceptions regarding eligibility for minimum essential coverage and eligibility for premium credits. An individual who is only eligible to obtain coverage through the individual (nongroup) health insurance market may be eligible to receive a premium credit. Also, an individual eligible for, but not enrolled in, an employer-sponsored plan may still be eligible for premium credits if the employer's coverage is either (1) not "affordable;" that is, the employee's premium contribution toward the employer's self-only plan would exceed 9.5% of household income;[19] or (2) does not provide "minimum value;" that is, the plan's payments cover less than 60% of total allowed costs on average.[20]

As shown in Figure 1, of the 29 million individuals projected by CBO to be enrolled in exchange coverage in 2019, approximately 1 million are projected to be enrolled because their employer's coverage is not "affordable."[21]

Individual's Employer Does Not Contribute toward Exchange Plan

Certain small employers (and in later years, potentially larger employers) may offer and contribute toward coverage through an exchange. If an individual is enrolled in an exchange through an employer who contributed toward that coverage, the individual will not be eligible for premium credits.[22]

Medicaid

Although ACA's Medicaid provisions are generally beyond the scope of this report, eligibility for Medicaid as expanded under ACA interacts with the provisions regarding premium credits for exchange coverage. From 2011 to 2013, states have the *option* to expand Medicaid to all non-elderly, non-pregnant individuals (i.e., childless adults and certain parents, except for those ineligible based on certain noncitizenship status) who are otherwise ineligible for Medicaid up to 133% FPL. Beginning in 2014, states with Medicaid programs will be *required* to extend Medicaid to these individuals.[23] In other words, the medical or family status of low-income individuals (pregnant, without children, etc.) will not matter for purposes of Medicaid eligibility. All non-elderly *citizens* (and certain *legal* aliens) with income up to 133% FPL will be eligible for Medicaid beginning in 2014. (ACA does not change noncitizens' eligibility for Medicaid.[24]) If a person who applied for premium credits in an exchange is determined to be eligible for Medicaid, the exchange must have them enrolled in Medicaid.[25]

POTENTIAL PREMIUM CONTRIBUTIONS AND PREMIUM CREDIT CALCULATIONS

The amount of the tax credit will vary from person to person: it depends on the household income of the taxpayer (and dependents), the premium for the exchange plan in which the taxpayer (and dependents) is (are) enrolled, and other factors. In certain instances, the credit amount may cover the entire premium and the taxpayer pays nothing towards the premium (see text box, scenario A). In other instances, the taxpayer may be required to pay part (or all) of the premium (see text box, scenario B).

Under scenario B, the amount that a taxpayer who receives a premium credit would be required to contribute towards the premium is capped as a percent of household income; that is, the *required premium contribution* would be the product of the taxpayer's household income and the "applicable percentage." In general, the applicable percentage will be less for those with lower incomes compared with those with higher incomes; where income is measured relative to the federal poverty level.

Under scenario B, the amount that taxpayers with income between 100% FPL and 133% FPL will be required to contribute towards the premium will be capped at 2 percent of household income. For taxpayers with income 300%-400% FPL, their premium contribution will be capped at 9.5% of income. ACA further specifies the applicable percentages that premium credit recipients, whose incomes are between those two income bands, would be required to pay towards the cost of exchange coverage under scenario B (see Figure 2).

Calculation of the *premium credit amount* (under scenario B) would be the arithmetic difference (if any) after subtracting the taxpayer's required premium contribution from the premium for the second lowest cost silver plan ("reference plan") available to the taxpayer. It is *theoretically* possible that a taxpayer's premium contribution could be equal to or exceed the premium for the reference plan, leaving that taxpayer with a premium credit amount of zero. Moreover, premium credit recipients who enroll in plans that are more expensive than the reference plan would have to pay the additional premium amount.

CALCULATION OF PREMIUM CREDIT AMOUNTS

The premium credit amount will be the lesser of either:

(A) The cost of the exchange plan that the taxpayer (and dependents) is (are) enrolled in; Or
(B) The excess, if any, resulting from the following formula:

The age-adjusted premium for the second lowest cost silver plan in the taxpayer's area,

Minus

The product of the taxpayer's household income and the "applicable percentage" (based on the taxpayer's household income relative to the federal poverty level).

PREMIUM CONTRIBUTION

If the premium credit amount (i.e., the lesser amount calculated above) is:

(A), then the taxpayer (and dependents) pay(s) nothing towards the premium for exchange coverage.
(B), then the individual (and dependents) pay(s) some (or all) of the premium for exchange coverage.

Illustrative Examples: If Premium Credits Were Available in 2011

For illustrative purposes only, if the premium credits were available in 2011, Table 2 shows annual income levels as measured against the 2011 FPL, by family size.

Table 2. Annual Income by 2011 Federal Poverty Level and Family Size For the 48 contiguous states and the District of Columbia

Federal Poverty Line (FPL)	Family Size			
	1	2	3	4
0%	$0	$0	$0	$0
50%	$5,445	$7,355	$9,265	$11,175
100%	$10,890	$14,710	$18,530	$22,350
133%	$14,484	$19,564	$24,645	$29,726
150%	$16,335	$22,065	$27,795	$33,525
200%	$21,780	$29,420	$37,060	$44,700
250%	$27,225	$36,775	$46,325	$55,875
300%	$32,670	$44,130	$55,590	$67,050
350%	$38,115	$51,485	$64,855	$78,225
400%	$43,560	$58,840	$74,120	$89,400

Source: CRS computation based on "Annual Update of the HHS Poverty Guidelines," 76 Federal Register 3637-3638, January 20, 2011, http://aspe.hhs.gov/poverty/11fedreg.pdf.

Notes: Under ACA, premium credits for eligible exchange coverage will not be available until 2014; the data in this table are for illustrative purposes only. Different income levels, as measured against the FPL, apply separately to Alaska and Hawaii (see "Annual Update of the HHS Poverty Guidelines" referenced under Source). The Federal Poverty Guidelines are updated annually for inflation.

Also for illustrative purposes, Table 3 displays the maximum *monthly* amounts that premium credit recipients would be required to contribute towards exchange coverage (provided that they enrolled in the reference plan or a less expensive exchange plan).

Both Figure 2 and Table 3 illustrate the "cliff effect" that occurs at 133% FPL. For those at or below 133% FPL who are not eligible for Medicaid but eligible for premium credits (e.g., certain legal permanent residents), the credits will ensure that such individuals pay no more than 2% of their income (if any) for exchange coverage.

Above 133% FPL, a formula is applied so that a family at 133.01% FPL will pay 3% of their income for those premiums. For example, as shown in Table 3, a family of four with income at 133% FPL ($29,726 in annual income) may be required to pay $50 in monthly premiums, if the exchange and premium credit provisions were currently in effect.

With one additional dollar of income ($29,727 in annual income), they would be required to pay $74 in monthly premiums. Thus, in this example, that additional $1 in income would lead to $24 more in required premium payments for the family per month (an additional $288 in premium contributions for the year). Some might observe that prior to the implementation of the ACA premium credits in 2014, an even larger cliff exists for citizens and qualified aliens, whose extra dollar of income makes them ineligible for Medicaid, at which point *no* premium credits were available.

Table 3. Maximum Monthly Premium Contributions, by Family Size, If Premium Credits were Available in 2011 (for the 48 contiguous states and the District of Columbia)

Federal Poverty Line (FPL)	Maximum Premium Contribution as a % of Income "Applicable Percentages")	Maximum Monthly Premium Contribution (2011), by Family Size			
		1	2	3	4
100%	2.0%	$18	$25	$31	$37
133.00%	2.0%	$24	$33	$41	$50
133.01%	3.0%	$36	$49	$62	$74
150%	4.0%	$54	$74	$93	$112
200%	6.3%	$114	$154	$195	$235
250%	8.05%	$183	$247	$311	$375
300%	9.5%	$259	$349	$440	$531
350%	9.5%	$302	$408	$513	$619
400%	9.5%	$345	$466	$587	$708

Source: CRS computation based on "Annual Update of the HHS Poverty Guidelines," 76 Federal Register 3637-3638, January 20, 2011, and ACA.

Notes: Under ACA, premium credits for eligible exchange coverage will not be available until 2014; the data in this table are for illustrative purposes only. Different income levels, as measured against the FPL, apply separately to Alaska and Hawaii (see "Annual Update of the HHS Poverty Guidelines" referenced under Source).

The Federal Poverty Guidelines are updated annually for inflation. If individuals enroll in more expensive plans than the second lowest-cost silver plan in their respective areas, they would be responsible for the additional premium amounts. The premium contribution amounts are rounded to the nearest dollar.

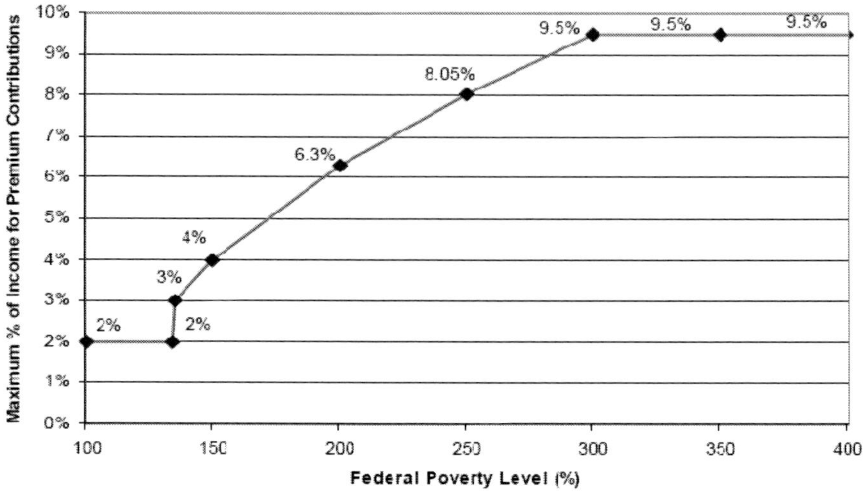

Source: CRS analysis of ACA.

Note: Beginning in 2014, citizens and qualifying legal residents with household income at or below 133% FPL will be eligible for Medicaid rather than premium credits.

Figure 2. Maximum Percentage of Income, as Measured by FPL, to go towards Premium Contributions.

Examples of Premium Credits for Self-Only and Family Coverage

For illustrative purposes, assume that premium credits were available in 2011. The following examples were calculated using the formula specified in ACA (see Table 4).[26] The examples assume that the individual or family is/are enrolled in an exchange plan with a premium that exceeds the amount of the premium credit they would receive, and therefore the credit would be based on the reference plan in the local area.

Note that the premium credit amounts are greater for those at the lower end of the eligible income range. The credit amount goes to zero when income is at 400% FPL.

Self-Only Coverage Examples

Assume that the annual premium for the reference plan (second lowest-cost silver plan) is $5,000 for self-only coverage (see Table 4). An individual with income at 200% FPL ($21,780 for 2011), would have a required annual contribution of $1,372 (i.e., $21,780 annual income multiplied by 6.3%). This individual would receive a tax credit of $3,628 for that year (i.e., $5,000 annual premium minus $1,372 required annual contribution), provided that the individual enrolled in an exchange plan with an annual premium that exceeds the credit amount.[27]

Assuming the same $5,000 annual premium for self-only coverage, an individual with income at 350% FPL would be required to contribute $3,621, resulting in a premium credit of $1,379.

Table 4. Annual Premium Contributions and Annual Premium Credit Amounts, if Credits were Available in 2011, by Coverage Tier

Coverage Tiers	Federal Poverty Level (FPL)	Income Levels based on FPL	Maximum Premium Contribution as a % of Income	Annual Premium	Required Annual Contribution	Annual Credit Amount
Self-Only	100%[a]	$10,890	2.0%	$5,000	$218	$4,782
	200%	$21,780	6.3%	$5,000	$1,372	$3,628
	350%	$38,115	9.5%	$5,000	$3,621	$1,379
	400%	N/A	N/A	N/A	N/A	$0
Family of Four	100%	$22,350	2.0%	$13,500	$447	$13,053
	200%	$44,700	6.3%	$13,500	$2,816	$10,684
	350%	$78,225	9.5%	$13,500	$7,431	$6,069
	400%	N/A	N/A	N/A	N/A	$0

Source: CRS computation based on "Annual Update of the HHS Poverty Guidelines," 76 Federal Register 3637-3638, January 20, 2011; KFF/HRET, "Employer Health Benefits 2011 Annual Survey," 2011; and ACA.

Notes: Under ACA, premium credits for eligible exchange coverage will not be available until 2014; the data in this table are for illustrative purposes only. Different income levels, as measured against the FPL, apply separately to Alaska and Hawaii (see "Annual Update of the HHS Poverty Guidelines" referenced under Source). The Federal Poverty Guidelines are updated annually for inflation.

a. Most individuals/families with income between 100% and 133% FPL will qualify for Medicaid. However, certain individuals will not: certain legal permanent residents (LPRs) who have resided in the U.S. less than five years. For purposes of the premium credit calculation, the income of credit-eligible LPRs will be assumed to be equivalent to 100% FPL.

Family Coverage Examples

The examples discussed above for self-only coverage may be replicated for purposes of estimating contributions and credit amounts for family coverage. Assume the annual premium for the second lowest-cost silver plan is $13,500 for family coverage (see Table 4). A family of four with income at 200% FPL ($44,700 for 2011), would have a required annual contribution of $2,816 (i.e., $44,700 multiplied by 6.3%). This family would receive a tax credit of $10,684 for that year (i.e., $13,500 minus $2,816).

Assuming the same $13,500 annual premium for family coverage, a family of four with income at 350% FPL would be required to contribute $7,431, resulting in a premium credit of $6,069.

Reconciliation of Premium Credits

Under ACA, the amount received in premium credits is based on the prior year's income tax returns. These amounts are reconciled in the next year when individuals file a tax return for the actual year in which they received a premium credit. If a tax filing unit's income changes, and the filer should have received a higher amount, this additional credit would be included in their tax refund for the year. On the other hand, any excess amount that was overpaid in premium credits would have to be repaid to the federal government as a tax payment. However, ACA imposed a limitation on the excess amount repaid for certain households. Specifically, for households with incomes below 400% of the FPL, the amount of repayment cannot exceed $400 (joint filers) and $250 (single filers). This amount will be indexed by inflation in future years.

Since the enactment of ACA, these limits have been increased in order to raise revenues for other legislative initiatives. On December 15, 2010, the Medicare and Medicaid Extenders Act of 2010 (P.L. 111-309) froze Medicare payments for physicians at 2010 rates (instead of the substantial, scheduled payment reduction).[28] The law also included several technical changes to extend existing programs that were scheduled to expire at the end of the year. To offset the cost from these changes, the bill changed the repayment limit for overpayment of premium credits to vary by income class (see Table 4).

On April 14, 2011, the Comprehensive 1099 Taxpayer Protection and Repayment of Exchange Subsidy Overpayment Act of 2011 (P.L. 112-9) was passed. The law repealed provisions in ACA that expanded the income reporting requirements to certain businesses.[29] To raise revenues to pay for these changes, the law lowered the maximum applicable limits for repayment of excess amount paid in premium credits to those shown in Table 6. In addition, those with household income of more than 400% of the FPL and up to 500% of FPL (at the time they filed their tax returns) were no longer subject to caps on repayment of overpayment amounts.

Most recently, on June 7, 2012, the House passed H.R. 436, the Health Care Cost Reduction Act of 2012, which would repeal an ACA provision that imposed a 2.3% excise tax on manufacturers and importers of a broad range of medical devices. H.R. 436 would also loosen some of the current restrictions on health flexible spending accounts.[30] To raise revenues for these provisions, H.R. 436 includes a measure that would remove all limits on repayment of overpayments of the premium credit, making individuals fully liable for the full amount of any overpayment.

According to the CBO, this change will raise $31.9 billion in revenues over 10 years (20132022).[31] The bill will now be sent to the Senate for consideration.

Table 5. Limits on Repayment of Excess Premium Credits Enacted by the Medicare and Medicaid Extenders Act (P.L. 111-309)

If the Household Income (Expressed as a Percentage of Poverty Line) Is:	The Applicable Dollar Limit for Joint Filers Is:
Less than 200%	$600
At least 200% but less than 250%	$1,000
At least 250% but less than 300%	$1,500
At least 300% but less than 350%	$2,000
At least 350% but less than 400%	$2,500
At least 400% but less than 450%	$3,000
At least 450% but less than 500%	$3,500

Note: The applicable dollar limit for single filers is 50% of the joint filer limit.

Table 6. Limits on Repayment of Excess Premium Credits Enacted by the Comprehensive 1099 Taxpayer Protection and Repayment of Exchange Subsidy Overpayment Act of 2011 (P.L. 112-9)

If the Household Income (Expressed as a Percentage of Poverty Line) Is:	The Applicable Dollar Limit for Married Filers Is:
Less than 200%	$600
At least 200% but less than 300%	$1,500
At least 300% but less than 400%	$2,500

Note: The applicable dollar limit for single filers is 50% of the joint filer limit.

Appendix. Health Insurance "Affordability" in the Exchange

While there is no widely accepted definition of individual "affordability" when it comes to health insurance premiums, and other health-care related out-of-pocket costs,[32] ACA sets insurance premium credits for persons, and their covered dependents, such that individuals and families will be required to spend no more than a specified percentage of income on premiums for specified health insurance plans in an exchange. Insurance premium credits under ACA will extend to individuals and families with modified adjusted gross income (hereinafter referred to simply as "income" with respect to ACA) between 100% and 400% FPL. ACA will provide premium credit support scaled to individual and family income relative to poverty such that eligible families' and individuals' premium contributions will be limited from 2.0% to 9.5% of income. Individuals and families with income at or above 400% of poverty will be ineligible for premium credits.

In terms of the premiums, ACA implicitly sets a pre-tax "affordability cap" of 9.5% of income on base coverage plans in the exchange (i.e., plans with a beginning actuarial value of 70%, not including the impact of cost-sharing subsidies), for individuals and families with income up to 400% of poverty. This section examines only the relative "affordability" of enrollee premiums in health insurance exchanges as a percentage of enrollee's income (adjusted gross income or AGI),[33] considering illustrative plan premiums, after subsidies and, if applicable, any federal tax deduction due to excess medical (i.e., qualifying health insurance and health care) expenses.

The insurance premiums used in the examples are for purposes of illustration only. Ultimately, the premiums individuals would face in the health insurance exchanges will depend on a host of factors, including the varying prices paid by plans for medical goods and services, the breadth of the provider network, the provisions regarding how out-of-network care is paid for (or not), the use of tools by the plan to reduce health care utilization (e.g., prior authorization for certain tests), and other factors.

The estimates shown here are based on illustrative premiums developed by the Kaiser Family Foundation (KFF) in 2009.[34] The illustrated plans are estimated to have a 70% actuarial value, meaning that the plans are expected to cover 70% of plan members' covered health care costs, with members' spending on cost-sharing (e.g., deductibles and copayments) covering the remaining 30%.

Based on Illustrated Annual Insurance Plan Cost for a 50-Year-Old with Single Coverage in a Medium-Cost Area ($5,428)

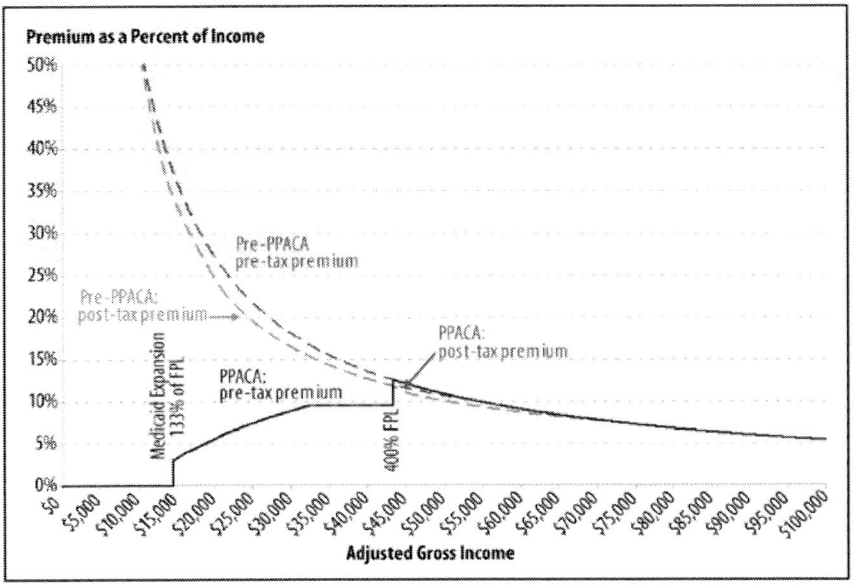

Source: Prepared by CRS based on Kaiser Family Foundation (KFF) illustrative health insurance premiums, for plans with an estimated actuarial value of 70%, in 2009.

Notes: Estimates are for illustration only, based on illustrated KFF health insurance premiums. Actual premiums would likely vary among health insurance exchanges based on a wide range of factors. The figure shows that prior to ACA, no premium credits are provided to individuals under 400% FPL, with the only federal subsidy being the effect of the deduction of medical expenses in excess of the 7.5% AGI threshold (as illustrated by the post-tax premium). ACA provides premium credits up to 400% of FPL, but increases the excess medical expense deduction threshold to 10.0% of AGI.

Figure A-1. ACA Compared to Pre-ACA Premiums: Pre- and Post-tax Out-of-Pocket Premiums as a Percentage of Adjusted Gross Income.

In the exchanges, insurers will be allowed to age-rate premiums within prescribed bands—under ACA, the highest age-adjusted premium can be no more than three times the lowest age-adjusted premium. ACA also will allow premiums to vary by tobacco use (by no more than 1.5:1 ratio) and geographic area.

Figure A-1 depicts the relative “affordability” of health insurance premiums prior to the application of the credits and ACA as of 2014, depicting out-of-pocket premiums as a percentage of income. The figure is based on

KFF's illustrated health insurance plan cost of $5,428 for a 50-year-old with single coverage living in a medium-cost area. Out-of-pocket premiums are shown based on pre-tax as well as post-tax premiums, using the excess medical expense threshold limit of 7.5% of adjusted gross income prior to ACA, and 10.0% after ACA.

The figure shows that at 100% of poverty, the illustrated insurance plan would cost individuals *half* of their pre-tax income prior to ACA—insurance premiums at this level, amounting to 50% of pre-tax income, would be considered unaffordable by many, and could crowd out spending on other basic needs such as food, shelter and utilities, and clothing.

Prior to ACA, the 7.5% excess medical expense deduction was the only federal subsidy toward the cost of their medical insurance that these individuals were eligible to receive; at lower-income levels the deduction had little or no effect on net post-tax premiums.

Under ACA, Medicaid will be expanded to 133% FPL, which will permit individuals to enroll with relatively limited or no premiums and cost-sharing. Under the depicted plan, health insurance premiums after reflecting ACA's subsidies would range from 3% of income at just above 133% of poverty, up to 9.5% of income at just under 400% FPL. At 400% FPL, individuals are shown bearing the full pre-tax cost of the illustrated plan ($5,428), which would amount to 12.5% of their pre-tax income; after applying the excess medical expense deduction under current law, the post-tax premium amounts to 11.7% of adjusted gross (pre-tax) income.

Illustrated Potential Effects of Age-Banding and Area Cost Adjustments on "Affordability"

Table A-1 shows illustrative KFF plan premiums in the exchange based on 2009 plan costs.[35] The examples shown here reflect the possible effects of age-banding of premiums and geographic cost variation on health insurance premium affordability.

In the examples shown, KFF illustrative premiums in higher-cost areas are set at 20% above those in medium-cost areas, and premiums in lower-cost areas are set 20% below.

Under KFF's age-banding, premiums for 30-year-olds are only slightly above those of 20-year-olds. At age 40, premiums are one-third higher than at age 20; at age 50, just over twice; and at age 60, three times as high (consistent with the age-banding limits). KFF estimates single+1 premiums as simply twice those of single coverage. Premiums for a family of four follow a similar age progression, except at age 50, premiums are only 84% higher than for 20-year-olds, and for 60-year-olds, 1.6 times higher.[36] Further discussion will focus on single individuals and couples (married and unmarried) under single premium and single+1 premium plans.

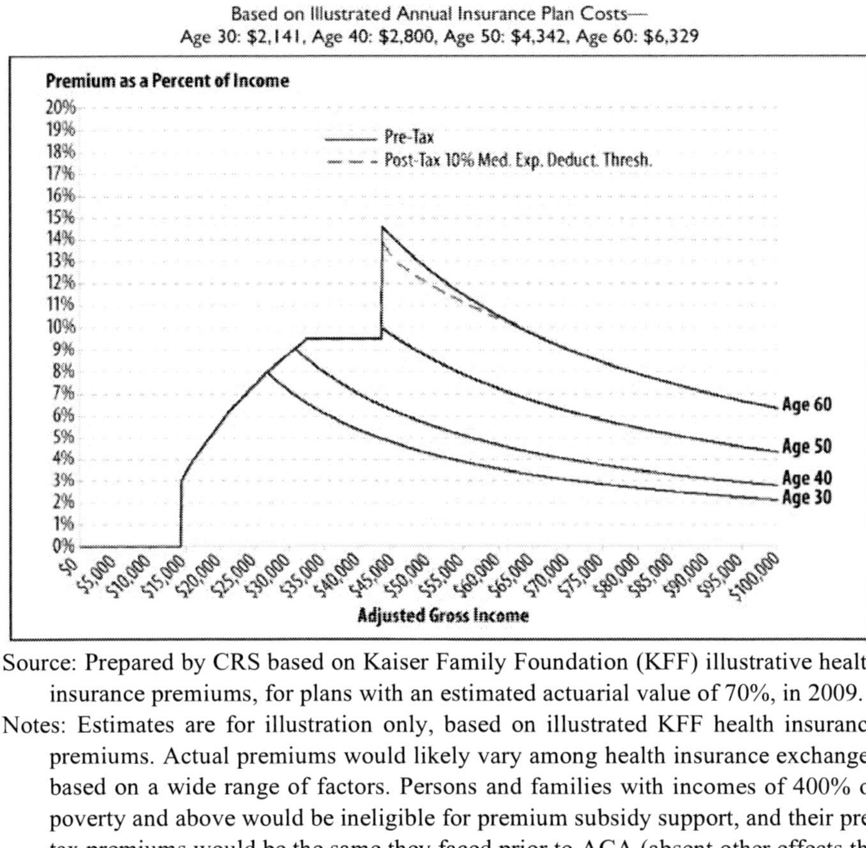

Source: Prepared by CRS based on Kaiser Family Foundation (KFF) illustrative health insurance premiums, for plans with an estimated actuarial value of 70%, in 2009.

Notes: Estimates are for illustration only, based on illustrated KFF health insurance premiums. Actual premiums would likely vary among health insurance exchanges based on a wide range of factors. Persons and families with incomes of 400% of poverty and above would be ineligible for premium subsidy support, and their pre-tax premiums would be the same they faced prior to ACA (absent other effects the law might have on reducing the price of health insurance). Net post-tax premiums are based ACA's excess medical expense deduction threshold of 10.0%.

Figure A-2. ACA: Pre- and Post-Tax Out-of-Pocket Premiums as a Percentage of Adjusted Gross Income, by Age—Single Policy in a Lower-Cost Area.

Table A-1. ACA: Illustrative Health Insurance Premiums, by Enrollee Age, Geographic Cost, and Plan Type, 2009

Age	Single premium			Single+1 premium			Family of four premium		
	Lower-cost area	Medium-cost area	Higher-cost area	Lower-cost area	Medium-cost area	Higher-cost area	Lower-cost area	Medium-cost area	Higher-cost area
20	$2,110	$2,637	$3,165	$4,220	$5,274	$6,330	$5,687	$7,108	$8,530
30	$2,141	$2,676	$3,211	$4,282	$5,352	$6,422	$6,290	$7,862	$9,435
40	$2,800	$3,500	$4,200	$5,600	$7,000	$8,400	$7,548	$9,435	$11,321
50	$4,342	$5,428	$6,513	$8,684	$10,856	$13,026	$10,489	$13,112	$15,734
60	$6,329	$7,911	$9,494	$12,658	$15,822	$18,988	$14,960	$18,700	$22,440

Source: Prepared by CRS from Kaiser Family Foundation (KFF) illustrative health insurance premiums, for plans with an estimated actuarial value of 70%, in 2009. Available online at http://healthreform.kff.org/SubsidyCalculator.aspx, accessed on March 23, 2010.

Note: Estimates are for illustration only. Illustrated premiums reflect a 3:1 age-banding, with premiums of oldest enrollees being three times those of youngest enrollees. Illustrated premiums in lower-cost areas are 20% lower than in medium-cost areas, and in higher-cost areas, 20% higher. Actual premiums will likely vary among health insurance exchanges based on a wide range of factors.

Table A-2 shows the illustrative KFF plan premiums as a percentage of income at 400% of the FPL, the point at which an individual or family no longer is eligible for premium subsidies under ACA. The table shows, for example, that 20- to 40-year-olds in the illustrated single plans have premiums ranging from 4.9% of income (for the youngest group in lower-cost areas), up to 8.1% for 40-year-olds in medium-cost areas—all below the ACA's implicit 9.5% affordability limit. For 40-year-olds in higher-cost areas, illustrated premiums (9.7% of income) are slightly above the law's affordability limit. For 50- and 60-year-olds, the illustrated premiums are above the 9.5% affordability limit in all markets, ranging from 10.0% to 15.0% of income for 50-year-olds, and 14.6% to 21.9% of income for 60-year-olds.[37]

Table A-2. ACA: Illustrative Health Insurance Premiums as a Percentage of Income at an Income Level of 400% of the Federal Poverty Level, by Enrollee Age, Geographic Cost, and Plan Type, 2009

Age	Single premium[a]			Single+1 premium[b]			Family of four premium[c]		
	Lower-cost area	Medium-cost area	Higher-cost area	Lower-cost area	Medium-cost area	Higher-cost area	Lower-cost area	Medium-cost area	Higher-cost area
20	4.9%	6.1%	7.3%	7.2%	9.0%	***10.9%***	6.4%	8.1%	9.7%
30	4.9%	6.2%	7.4%	7.3%	9.2%	***11.0%***	7.1%	8.9%	10.7%
40	6.5%	8.1%	***9.7%***	***9.6%***	***12.0%***	***14.4%***	*8.6%*	***10.7%***	***12.8%***
50	***10.0%***	***12.5%***	***15.0%***	***14.9%***	***18.6%***	22.4%	***11.9%***	***14.9%***	***17.8%***
60	***14.6%***	***18.3%***	***21.9%***	***21.7%***	***27.1%***	32.6%	***17.0%***	***21.2%***	***25.4%***

Source: Prepared by CRS based on Kaiser Family Foundation (KFF) illustrative health insurance premiums, for plans with an estimated actuarial value of 70%, in 2009. Available online at http://healthreform.kff.org/ SubsidyCalculator.aspx, accessed on March 23, 2010.

Note: Estimates are for illustration only, based on illustrated KFF health insurance premiums. Actual premiums will likely vary among health insurance exchanges based on a wide range of factors. Values in ***bold italic*** are above ACA's premium cap of 9.5% of income, extending up to 400% of FPL.

a. Premium as a percentage of income based on 400% of FPL for a single person ($43,320).

b. Premium as a percentage of income based on 400% of FPL for a 2-person family ($58,280).

c. Premium as a percentage of income based on 400% of FPL for a 4-person family ($88,200).

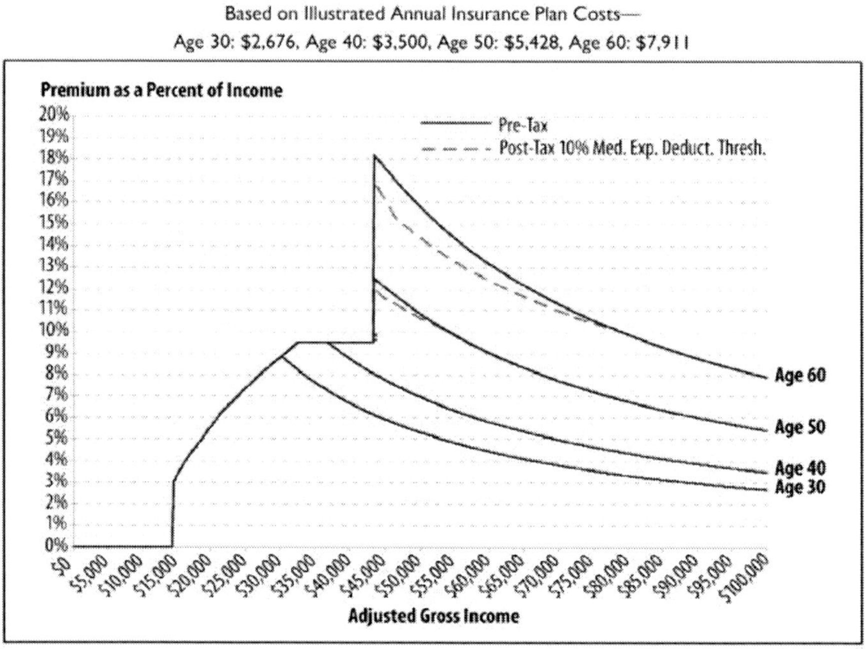

Source: Prepared by CRS based on Kaiser Family Foundation (KFF) illustrative health insurance premiums, for plans with an estimated actuarial value of 70%, in 2009.

Notes: Estimates are for illustration only, based on illustrated KFF health insurance premiums. Actual premiums would likely vary among health insurance exchanges based on a wide range of factors. Persons and families with incomes of 400% of poverty and above would be ineligible for premium subsidy support, and their pre-tax premiums would be the same they faced prior to ACA (absent other effects the law might have on reducing the price of health insurance). Net post-tax premiums are based ACA's excess medical expense deduction threshold of 10.0%.

Figure A-3.ACA: Pre- and Post-Tax Out-of-Pocket Premiums as a Percentage of Adjusted Gross Income, by Age—Single Policy in a Medium-Cost Area.

Figure A-2 through Figure A-4 depict pre- and post-tax premiums as a percentage of income under illustrated self-coverage plans, by enrollee age, in lower-cost, medium-cost, and higher-cost areas, respectively. Figure A-2, for example, shows that under the illustrated premiums for a lower-cost area all enrollees with incomes below 400% of poverty would have pre-tax premiums amounting to less than 9.5% income—ACA's affordability cap—due to the law's premium credits. However, the impact of age-rating premiums will differ for younger vs. older individuals, as their income increases. For example, for individuals age 30 and 40, the illustrated premiums as a percentage of income naturally decline before reaching the 400% FPL, because they face relatively low premiums (compared with older individuals) as their income increases.

In contrast, individuals age 40 and 50 face higher exchange premiums and benefit from the 9.5% income affordability cap all the way up to the 400% income-eligibility limit. At 400% of poverty, illustrated premiums for the 50-year-olds increase slightly, to 10.0% of income, and for 60-year-olds, more substantially, to 14.6% of income.

Based on Illustrative Annual Insurance Plan Costs—
Age 30: $3,211, Age 40: $4,200, Age 50: $6,513, Age 60: $9,494

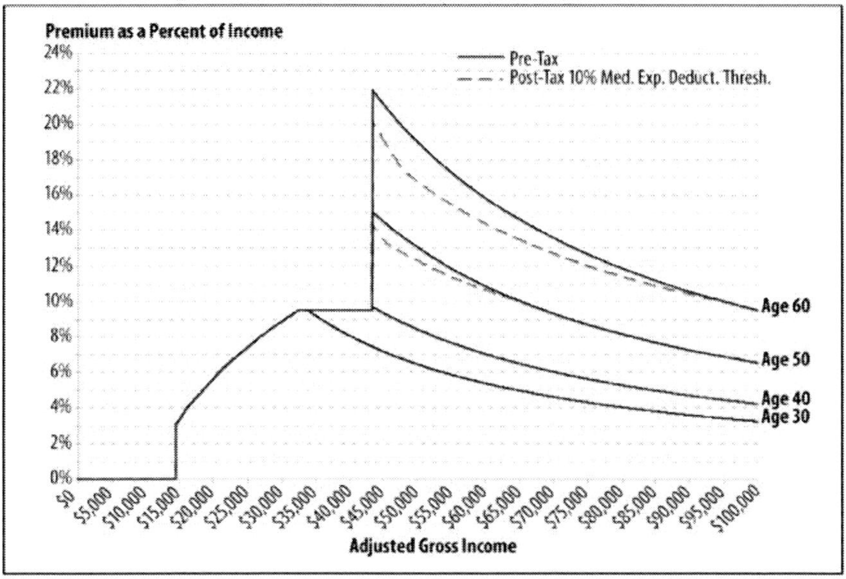

Source: Prepared by CRS based on Kaiser Family Foundation (KFF) illustrative health insurance premiums, for plans with an estimated actuarial value of 70%, in 2009.

Notes: Estimates are for illustration only, based on illustrated KFF health insurance premiums. Actual premiums would likely vary among health insurance exchanges based on a wide range of factors. Persons and families with incomes of 400% of poverty and above would be ineligible for premium subsidy support, and their pre-tax premiums would be the same they faced prior to ACA (absent other effects the law might have on reducing the price of health insurance). Net post-tax premiums are based ACA's excess medical expense deduction threshold of 10.0%.

Figure A-4. ACA: Pre- and Post-Tax Out-of-Pocket Premiums as a Percentage of Adjusted Gross Income, by Age—Single Policy in a Higher-Cost Area.

In medium-cost areas, illustrated in Figure A-3, pre-tax premiums for 50-year-olds amount to 12.5% of income, and for 60-year-olds, 18.3% at 400% of the FPL. In higher-cost areas, illustrated in Figure A-4, pre-tax premiums at 400% of poverty amount to 15% of income for 50-year-olds, and 21.9% of income for 60-year-olds. For 60-year-olds, pre-tax premiums fall back to 9.5% of income once income reaches $99,937 or 923% FPL.

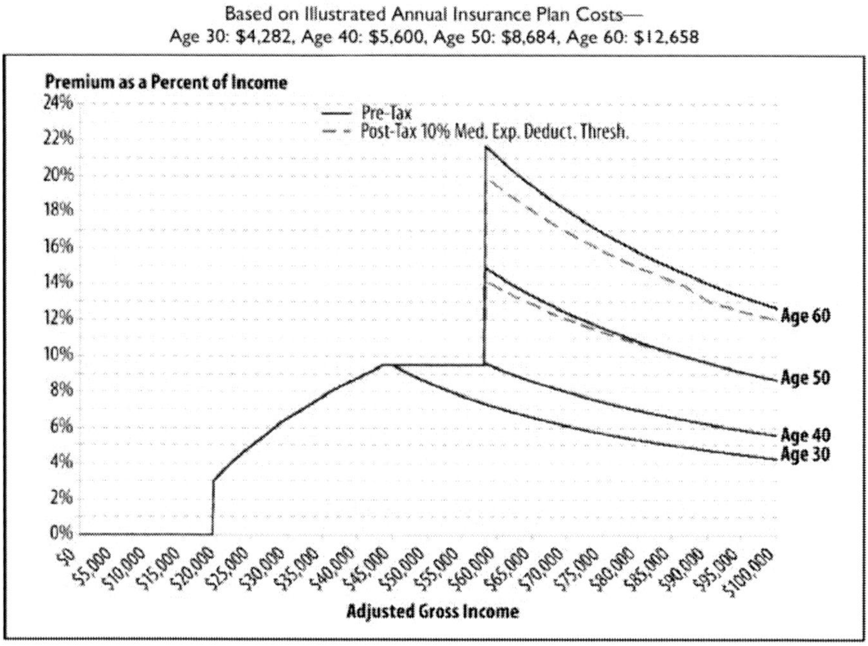

Source: Prepared by CRS based on Kaiser Family Foundation (KFF) illustrative health insurance premiums, for plans with an estimated actuarial value of 70%, in 2009.

Notes: Estimates are for illustration only, based on illustrated KFF health insurance premiums. Actual premiums would likely vary among health insurance exchanges based on a wide range of factors. Persons and families with incomes of 400% of poverty and above would be ineligible for premium subsidy support, and their pre-tax premiums would be the same they faced prior to ACA (absent other effects the law might have on reducing the price of health insurance). Net post-tax premiums are based ACA's excess medical expense deduction threshold of 10.0%.

Figure A-5. ACA: Pre- and Post-Tax Out-of-Pocket Premiums as a Percentage of Adjusted Gross Income, by Age—Married Couple with no Children, Single+1 Policy in a Lower-Cost Area.

Based on Illustrated Annual Insurance Plan Costs—
Age 30: $5,352, Age 40: $7,000, Age 50: $10,856, Age 60: $15,822

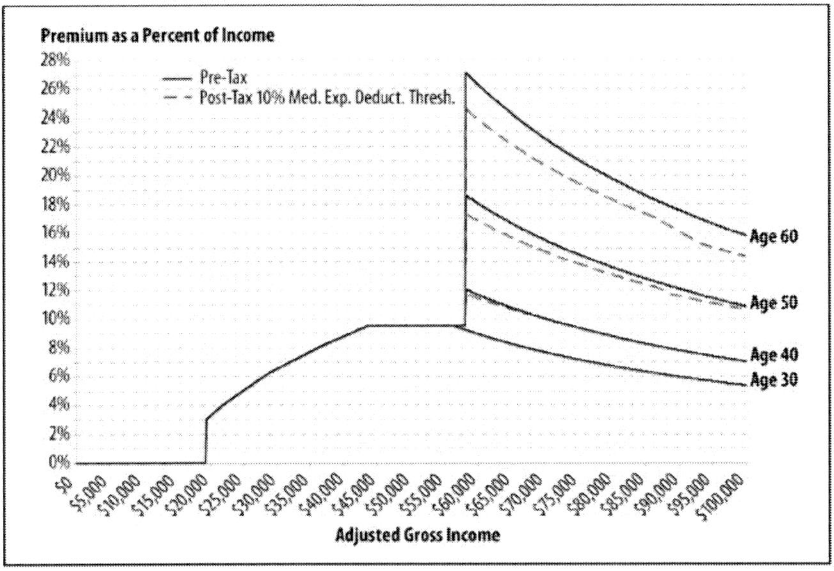

Source: Prepared by CRS based on Kaiser Family Foundation (KFF) illustrative health insurance premiums, for plans with an estimated actuarial value of 70%, in 2009.

Notes: Estimates are for illustration only, based on illustrated KFF health insurance premiums. Actual premiums would likely vary among health insurance exchanges based on a wide range of factors. Persons and families with incomes of 400% of poverty and above would be ineligible for premium subsidy support, and their pre-tax premiums would be the same they faced prior to ACA (absent other effects the law might have on reducing the price of health insurance). Net post-tax premiums are based ACA's excess medical expense deduction threshold of 10.0%.

Figure A-6. ACA: Pre- and Post-Tax Out-of-Pocket Premiums as a Percentage of Adjusted Gross Income, by Age—Married Couple with no Children, Single+1 Policy in a Medium-Cost Area.

Figure A-5 through Figure A-7 depict pre- and post-tax premiums as a percentage of income under illustrated plans, for a married couple with no children having "single+1" insurance coverage, by enrollee age, in three geographic cost areas. The illustrated premiums for "single+1" coverage are twice those for single coverage. Table A-2 shows that for a married couple with a single+1 policy, at 400% of poverty, illustrated premiums in lower-cost areas for 50- and 60-year-olds are well above the 9.5% "affordability threshold" with illustrated premiums at 14.9% of income for 50-year-olds, and

21.7% for 60-year-olds. In medium-cost areas, illustrated premiums at 400% of poverty for a 40-year-old (12.0% of income) are above the 9.5% "affordability threshold," and range up to 27.1% of income for 60-year-olds. For married-couples in higher-cost areas, illustrated premiums at 400% of poverty are higher than the 9.5% "affordability threshold" at all ages, ranging from 10.9% of income for a 20-year-old, up to 32.6% for 60-year-old enrollees.

Based on Illustrated Annual Insurance Plan Costs—
Age 30: $6,422, Age 40: $8,400, Age 50: $13,026, Age 60: $18,988

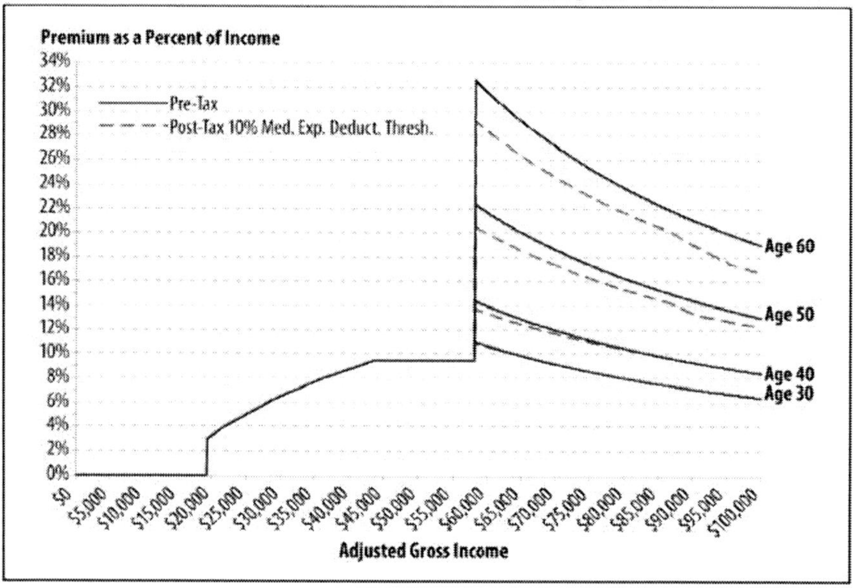

Source: Prepared by CRS based on Kaiser Family Foundation (KFF) illustrative health insurance premiums, for plans with an estimated actuarial value of 70%, in 2009.

Notes: Estimates are for illustration only, based on illustrated KFF health insurance premiums. Actual premiums would likely vary among health insurance exchanges based on a wide range of factors. Persons and families with incomes of 400% of poverty and above would be ineligible for premium subsidy support, and their pre-tax premiums would be the same they faced prior to ACA (absent other effects the law might have on reducing the price of health insurance). Net post-tax premiums are based ACA's excess medical expense deduction threshold of 10.0%.

Figure A-7. ACA: Pre- and Post-Tax Out-of-Pocket Premiums as a Percentage of Adjusted Gross Income, by Age—Married Couple with no Children, Single+1 Policy in a Higher-Cost Area.

It should be noted that the figures that follow reflect estimates under ACA only, unlike Figure A-1, which illustrates pre- and post-tax premiums both before and after ACA.

Relative "Affordability" of Premiums for Married and Unmarried Couples

Some have described the structure of the premium support provided under ACA's health insurance exchanges, with respect to the phase out of premium support relative to enrollees' income, as resulting in a "marriage penalty."[38] Under ACA's health insurance exchanges, a couple may receive a lesser subsidy, and consequently incur higher out-of-pocket insurance premiums, if they are married, as opposed to unmarried, all other things being equal, thus resulting in a "marriage penalty."[39] ACA phases out premium support on the basis of income relative to the Federal Poverty Level. Premium support in the exchanges for a married couple would be based on their combined income relative to the FPL for two persons ($14,570), and if unmarried, based on their individual incomes relative to the FPL for one person ($10,830). Because the FPL for the married couple is not twice that of a single person, but only 35% higher (i.e., $14,570/$10,830), premium support phases out at a faster rate for the married couple than for the unmarried couple, with equal incomes and combined (pre-subsidy) insurance plan costs. If married, the couple would be ineligible for premium support in the exchange once their income reaches $58,280 (i.e., 400% of the FPL), but if unmarried, premium support could potentially be retained until each individual's income reaches 400% for a single person ($43,320), or potentially until their combined income reaches $86,640 (which would be 595% FPL for a married couple).[40]

The FPL, as originally constructed, recognized that while two persons cannot live as cheaply as one, they can live more cheaply living together, than living apart. In other words, there are economic gains that result from "economies of scale" from living jointly, rather than apart. "Marriage penalties" can result to the extent that FPLs assign lower cost to each additional family member, regardless of whether that family member is a spouse, children, etc.[41] In addition, "marriage penalties" may result more directly from the definition of the economic unit to which the FPL, or other income criteria, is applied.[42] Following are two examples of other federal programs that illustrate how the definition of the economic unit can affect couples' eligibility.

Many federal programs use the FPL as the basis for determining eligibility, setting benefit levels, and phasing out benefits. For example, the Supplemental Nutrition Assistance Program (SNAP) (formerly named the Food Stamp program) counts *household* income for purposes of determining household income eligibility. *Households* with gross income above 100% of poverty are ineligible for the program, as are *households* with net income (after certain disregards) above 130% of poverty. With respect to SNAP, a married couple is treated the same as an unmarried couple, if living together in the same *household*. So, in this context, there is no inherent "marriage penalty" in SNAP, even though it uses the FPL. However, there is a potential "penalty" for two persons living apart, where one or both are receiving SNAP benefits, if they choose to live together, as their combined household income might make them ineligible for SNAP benefits. However, by living together, rather than separately, two individuals, whether married or unmarried, could benefit from implied economies of scale.

In contrast, the Earned Income Tax Credit (EITC) may be said to have a "marriage penalty," even though it does not use the FPL to scale benefits. This is because two unrelated unmarried individuals are treated as individuals under the tax code (single filers), whereas if married their incomes are combined and they are treated as married joint filers.

With respect to the EITC, one or both individuals could be eligible for the EITC based on their individual earnings, if unmarried, but become ineligible, or receive a lesser benefit, if they were married, as the EITC would then be based on their combined earnings.

Figure A-8 and Figure A-9 compare premiums under ACA as a percentage of income for a married couple relative to an unmarried couple, in a medium-cost area, at age 30 and age 50, respectively. The figures show that premiums as a percentage of income would be higher for a married couple than if the couple were unmarried, even though their incomes and insurance premiums are the same.[43]

In the illustrated example at age 30 (Figure A-8), the difference in premiums between married and unmarried couples, and as a percentage of income, is much greater, as the married couple's premium subsidy phases out at a faster rate based on its income than it does for the unmarried couple based on their combined income.

In the illustration, the married couple no longer receives premium support once their income exceeds $56,337. At that point their premium as a percentage of income naturally falls below ACA's 9.5% "affordability cap," and they are deemed to no longer need premium subsidy support.

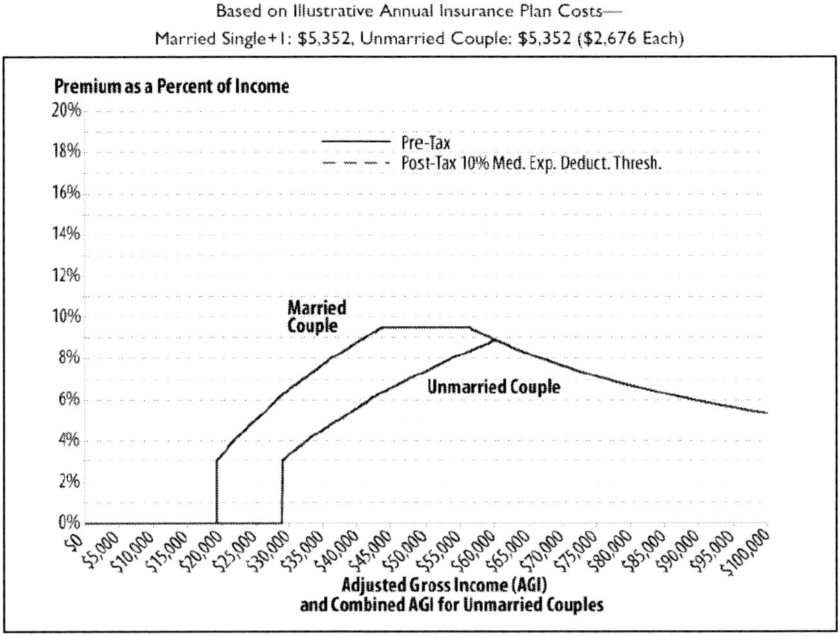

Source: Prepared by CRS based on Kaiser Family Foundation (KFF) illustrative health insurance premiums, for plans with an estimated actuarial value of 70%, in 2009.

Notes: Estimates are for illustration only, based on illustrated KFF health insurance premiums. Actual premiums would likely vary among health insurance exchanges based on a wide range of factors. Persons and families with incomes of 400% of poverty and above would be ineligible for premium subsidy support, and their pre-tax premiums would be the same they faced prior to ACA (absent other effects the law might have on reducing the price of health insurance). Net post-tax premiums are based ACA's excess medical expense deduction threshold of 10.0%. Under this example, gross premiums are below the 10% excess medical expense deduction threshold at all income levels.

Figure A-8. ACA: Pre- and Post-Tax Out-of-Pocket Premiums as a Percentage of Adjusted Gross Income, Comparison of Two Couples Age 30 (Married and Unmarried) in a Medium-Cost Area.

For the unmarried couple at the same combined income level, assuming their income is equally split, they are individually eligible for premium support of $326 each, based on their individual income ($28,168), and thereby would receive combined premium support of $652. In the example, the unmarried couple's combined premiums amount to 8.3% of their combined income, compared to 9.5% for their married counterpart.

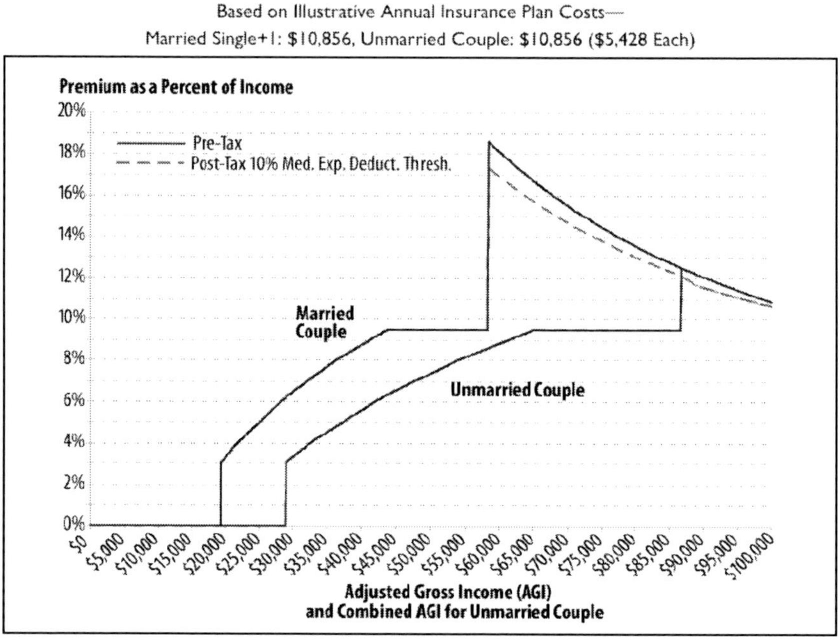

Source: Prepared CRS based on Kaiser Family Foundation (KFF) illustrative health insurance premiums, for plans with an estimated actuarial value of 70%, in 2009.

Notes: Estimates are for illustration only, based on illustrated KFF health insurance premiums. Actual premiums would likely vary among health insurance exchanges based on a wide range of factors. Persons and families with incomes of 400% of poverty and above would be ineligible for premium subsidy support, and their pre-tax premiums would be the same they faced prior to ACA (absent other effects the law might have on reducing the price of health insurance). Net post-tax premiums are based ACA's excess medical expense deduction threshold of 10.0%.

Figure A-9. ACA: Pre- and Post-Tax Out-of-Pocket Premiums as a Percentage of Adjusted Gross Income, Comparison of Two Couples Age 50 (Married and Unmarried) in a Medium-Cost Area.

The "marriage penalty" effect increases to the extent premiums exceed the 9.5% "affordability cap" at the point at which a married couple no longer qualifies for premium support (i.e., 400% of poverty, or $58,280). For example, for the 50-year-old couple depicted in Figure A-9, at an income level just below $58,280 (i.e., 400% of poverty for the married couple) their premium as a percentage of income is at the 9.5% cap if they are married and 8.6% if they are unmarried. However, the married couple loses premium subsidy support once their income reaches $58,280, and their premium nearly doubles, amounting to 18.6% of their income. In contrast, the unmarried couple continues to be eligible for premium support, at the same combined income level and plan cost as their married counterpart; their combined premiums amount to 8.6% of their combined income—less than half that of the married couple. In the example, both members of the unmarried couple would continue to receive premium support until their individual income reaches $43,320 (400% of the FPL for a single individual), which amounts to a combined income of $86,640. At that, and higher, combined income levels, the unmarried and married couples' premiums are identical, since neither would then qualify for premium credits.

CONCLUSION

Relative affordability of health insurance premiums individuals and families might face within health insurance exchanges will likely vary from exchange to exchange based on a host of factors. The examples shown in this report are for illustration only, depicting a range by which premiums might reasonably be expected to vary.

ACA will directly improve health insurance affordability for individuals and families with income up to 400% of poverty, by ensuring that no individual or family would pay more than 9.5% of their income for a health insurance plan with an actuarial value of 70% (not including the impact of cost-sharing subsidies). Additionally, ACA will extend Medicaid coverage to 133% of poverty for many individuals, which will permit them to enroll with relatively little or no premiums and cost-sharing. Persons and families with incomes of 400% of poverty and above will be ineligible for premium subsidy support, and their premiums will be the same they would have faced before ACA (absent other effects the law might have on reducing the price of health insurance). Individuals and families who are younger and/or who live in lower-cost areas, as opposed to higher-cost areas, may be able to find plans offered in the exchange costing 9.5% or less of income at some income ranges below 400% of poverty. Others might face exchange premiums that well exceed 9.5% of income, but due to ACA's premium subsidy support their premiums will be capped until their income reaches 400% of poverty. At that point, enrollees might incur abrupt, and in some cases substantial, increases in their health insurance premiums. Additionally, ACA raises the excess medical expense deduction threshold from 7.5% to 10.0% of AGI. Consequently, some individuals and families may find their post-tax insurance premiums to be higher after ACA than before, all other things being equal.

ACA phases out premium support subsidies based on individuals' or families' income relative to poverty. Because the FPL for the married couple is not twice that of a single person, but only 35% higher (i.e., $14,570/$10,830), premium support under ACA phases out at a faster rate relative to *income* for a married couple than it does for a single person, even though the phase-out rate relative to the FPL is the same. The structure of the phase-out results in what some might describe as a "marriage penalty." One or both individuals in a couple who are unmarried might be eligible for premium support subsidies based on their individual incomes, but if they married they might not, based on their combined income; if found eligible, the premium subsidy they might receive as a married couple could be less than the combined premium subsidies they might receive as an unmarried couple.

End Notes

[1] Certain individuals who qualify for premium credits will also qualify for cost-sharing subsidies to help pay for deductibles, copayments, etc. The cost-sharing subsidies are outside the scope of this report.

[2] *Federal Register,* Vol. 76, No. 159, August 17, 2011.

[3] Hereinafter, "ACA" will refer to P.L. 111-148, as amended.

[4] Exchanges are designed to offer nongroup policies and small group plans. Large groups may participate in exchanges, at state option, beginning in 2017.

[5] Actuarial value is a summary measure of a plan's generosity, expressed as the percentage of medical expenses estimated to be paid by the insuer for a standard population and set of allowed charges. The higher the percentage, the more generous the coverage.

[6] §412(a)(3).

[7] CBO letter to Speaker Pelosi, ACA cost estimate, March 20, 2010, p. 9 and Table 4, http://cbo.gov/ftpdocs/113xx/doc11379/AmendReconProp.pdf'sAmendmenttoReconciliationProposal.pdf.

[8] "Health Insurance Premium Tax Credit," 26 CFR Part 1, *Federal Register*, Vol. 76, No. 159, August 17, 2011, available online at http://www.gpo.gov/fdsys/pkg/FR-2011-08-17/pdf/2011-20728.pdf.

[9] §1412(a)(3).

[10] §1401, adding a new §36B(c)(2)(A)(i) to the Internal Revenue Code.

[11] §1312(f)(3). For more information about the treatment of noncitizens under ACA, see CRS Report R40889, *Noncitizen Eligibility and Verification Issues in the Health Care Reform Legislation*.

[12] The FPL used for public program eligibility varies by family size and by whether the individual resides in the 48 contiguous states and the District of Columbia versus Alaska or Hawaii. See "Annual Update of the HHS Poverty Guidelines," 76 *Federal Register* 3637-3638, January 20, 2011, http://aspe.hhs.gov/poverty/11fedreg.pdf.

[13] In Section 2002(a) and Section 1401(a) of ACA, household income is defined to be MAGI in compliance with the Internal Revenue Code (IRC). With respect to the federal tax code,

gross income is total income minus certain exclusions (e.g., public assistance payments, employer contributions to health insurance payments). From gross income, adjusted gross income (AGI) is calculated to reflect a number of deductions, including trade and business deductions, losses from sale of property, and alimony payments. MAGI is defined as AGI plus certain foreign earned income and tax-exempt interest. However, for premium credit eligibility purposes, the definition of MAGI will include non-taxable Social Security benefits (as amended in P.L. 112-56). For additional discussion about the use of MAGI with respect to ACA premium credits, see CRS Report R41997, *Definition of Income in ACA for Certain Medicaid Provisions and Premium Credits*.

[14] An exception is made for lawfully present aliens with income below 100% of the FPL, who are ineligible for Medicaid for the first five years that they are lawfully present. These taxpayers will be treated as though their income is exactly 100% of FPL for purposes of the premium credit.

[15] Given the interaction between the ACA's provisions on exchanges and Medicaid, most individuals with income between 100% and 133% FPL will be eligible for Medicaid, beginning in 2014. For additional information about the Medicaid provisions in the ACA, see CRS Report R41210, *Medicaid and the State Children's Health Insurance Program (CHIP) Provisions in ACA: Summary and Timeline.*

[16] The FPL used for public program eligibility, the Federal Poverty Guideline, varies by family size and by whether the individual resides in the 48 contiguous states and the District of Columbia versus Alaska or Hawaii. See "Annual Update of the HHS Poverty Guidelines," 76 Federal Register 3637-3638, January 20, 2011, http://aspe.hhs.gov/poverty/11fedreg.pdf.

[17] A grandfathered health plan is a group health plan or health insurance coverage (including coverage from the individual health insurance market) in which a person was enrolled on and since the date of enactment of ACA. For additional information about grandfathered plans, see CRS Report R41166, *Grandfathered Health Plans Under the Patient Protection and Affordable Care Act (ACA).*

[18] The Treasury Department, in the NPRM on premium credits, requested comments on the transition of individuals from exchange coverage to public coverage (such as Medicaid). The comment period ended on October 31, 2011, and a public hearing was held on November 17, 2011. *Federal Register*, Vol. 76, No. 159, Aug. 17, 2011.

[19] The Treasury Department, in the NPRM on premium credits, proposed an employee safe harbor that would allow an employee to be eligible for premium credits, even if the employer plan was later determined to be affordable. The comment period ended on October 31, 2011, and a public hearing was held on November 17, 2011. *Federal Register*, Vol. 76, No. 159, Aug. 17, 2011.

[20] §1401(a), adding a new §36B(c)(2)(C) to the Internal Revenue Code.

[21] CBO letter to Speaker Pelosi, ACA cost estimate, March 20, 2010, p. 9 and Table 4, http://www.cbo.gov/ftpdocs/113xx/doc11379/Manager'sAmendmenttoReconciliationProposal.pdf.

[22] §1401 of ACA, adding a new §36B(c)(2)(A)(ii) to the Internal Revenue Code.

[23] ACA specifies that an income disregard in the amount of 5% FPL will be used to determine Medicaid eligibility based on MAGI; thus the effective minimum income eligibility threshold for such individuals in this new eligibility group will be 138% FPL.

[24] As under law prior to ACA, certain lawfully present aliens are eligible for full Medicaid benefits (e.g., refugees, asylees, and some legal permanent residents (LPRs) who have been here at least five years) while others are not (e.g., certain LPRs who have been here less than five years).

[25] §1311(d)(4) and §1413(a).

[26] See the text box "Calculations of Premium Credit Amount" for the premium credit formula.

[27] According to ACA's premium credit provisions, in order for the credit amount to be based on the reference plan, the estimated credit amount must exceed the cost of the exchange plan in which the individual/family is enrolled.

[28] See CRS Report R40907, *Medicare Physician Payment Updates and the Sustainable Growth Rate (SGR) System*, by Jim Hahn and Janemarie Mulvey.

[29] See CRS Report R41782, *1099 Information Reporting Requirements and Penalties: Recent Legislative Activity*, by Carol A. Pettit and Edward C. Liu

[30] See CRS Report RL32656, *Health Care Flexible Spending Accounts*, by Janemarie Mulvey for more information.

[31] Congressional Budget Office, Cost Estimate for the Honorable David Dreier, Chairman, Committee on Rules, June 5, 2012.

[32] ACA includes provisions to study affordability issues. It requires GAO to conduct a survey of the cost and affordability of health care insurance provided under the exchanges for owners and employees of small business concerns, including data on enrollees in exchanges and individuals purchasing health insurance coverage outside of exchanges. GAO is also required to conduct a study on the affordability of health insurance coverage (including the impact of credits for individuals and small businesses), the availability of affordable health benefits plans (including a study of whether the percentage of household income used for credit purposes is appropriate for determining whether employer-provided coverage is affordable and whether such level may be lowered without significantly increasing the costs to the federal government and reducing employer-provided coverage), and the ability of individuals to maintain essential health benefits coverage. ACA also requires the HHS Secretary to conduct a study examining the feasibility and implication of adjusting the FPL for premium and cost-sharing credits for different geographic areas so as to reflect the variations in cost-of-living among different areas. If the Secretary determines that an adjustment is feasible, the study should include a methodology to make such an adjustment.

[33] While the definition of income for the purposes of premium credit eligibility uses MAGI, for ease of analysis the illustrations discussed in this section uses AGI as the definition of income.

[34] http://healthreform.kff.org/SubsidyCalculator.aspx, accessed on March 23, 2010.

[35] Given that KFF developed their illustrative premiums in 2009, the original analysis compared such amounts to the federal poverty levels applicable for that year. Since FPLs are adjusted annually, the FPLs used in the analysis in the Appendix of the paper are different from the FPLs used elsewhere in the report.

[36] Presumably the smaller difference for family coverage by age, compared to single coverage, is due to an assumption that by age 50, couples' children tend to be older than those of younger couples, and older children generally have lower health care utilization rates than younger children.

[37] One study found that annual premiums in the nongroup market for 60- to 64-year-olds averaged $5,755 in 2009, which would be 13.3% of income for an individual at 400% FPL. See Table 2, "Individual Health Insurance," AHIP Center for Policy and Research, October 2009.

[38] Martin Vaughan, "Married Couples Pay More than Unmarried Under Health Bill," *Wall Street Journal*, January 6, 2010, online edition. Available online at http://online.wsj.com/article/SB126281943134818675.html.

[39] The Treasury Department, in the NPRM on premium credits, requested comments on providing relief to individuals who would receive less premium support after they marry during the tax year. The comment period ended on October 31, 2011. *Federal Register*, Vol. 76, No. 159, Aug. 17, 2011.

[40] This assumes that the two members of the unmarried couple have individual incomes that are equal. For the married couple, it makes no difference how their income is split.

[41] The 2009 federal poverty levels were $10,830 for an individual, and $3,740 for each additional person.

[42] Because premium credit amounts under the exchanges will be scaled based on income relative to poverty, other types of individuals might find differences in their premiums depending on their living arrangements, other than just whether they're married or not. For example, the total premiums for a single parent with two older children (e.g., age 18 to 25) might differ depending on whether the children enroll separately, based on their individual income, or under the umbrella of a family policy, based on the parent's and children's combined income.

[43] For the 30-year-old couple, if they're married, $5,352 for a single+1 policy, and if they're unmarried, each with a $2,676 single policy, amounting to $5,352 combined. For the 50-year-old couple, if they're married, $10,586 for a single+1 policy, and if they're unmarried, each with a $5,428 single policy, amounting to $10,586 combined. The figures assume the two members of the unmarried couple have equal income. Results would differ if their income were split unequally. For the married couple, it makes no difference as to how their income is split.

In: Health Insurance Exchanges …
Editor: Edward J. Volpicelli
ISBN: 978-1-62417-367-7

Chapter 3

GENERAL GUIDANCE ON FEDERALLY-FACILITATED EXCHANGES*

Centers for Medicare and Medicaid Services

This document outlines the Department of Health and Human Services' (HHS) approach to implementing a Federally-facilitated Exchange (FFE) in any State where a State-based Exchange is not operating. In addition to describing our high-level operational approach, we discuss:

1. How States can partner with HHS to implement selected functions in an FFE,
2. Key policies organized by Exchange function, and
3. How HHS will consult with a variety of stakeholders to implement an FFE.

Subsequent guidance documents will include additional policy and operational details intended to inform State decision-making and preparation for Exchange participation, roles and responsibilities, and potential areas of collaboration.

---

* This is an edited, reformatted and augmented version of the Center for Consumer Information and Insurance Oversight, dated May 16, 2012.

I. BACKGROUND

The Affordable Care Act (P.L. 111-148 and 111-152) allows each State the opportunity to establish an Affordable Insurance Exchange ("Exchange") to help individuals and small employers purchase affordable health insurance coverage.

Exchanges will allow individuals and eligible employers to compare and select from qualified health plans (QHPs) for their families and their employees that meet benefit design, consumer protection, and other standards. Exchanges will increase access to coverage by providing a single point of access for individual consumers to receive eligibility determinations for enrollment in the Exchange and for insurance affordability programs, and select a QHP that best meets their needs.

By permitting consumers and employers to easily compare health plans, Exchanges will increase competition among issuers and improve the affordability of coverage. Exchanges are integral to the Affordable Care Act's goals of prohibiting discrimination against people with pre-existing conditions and insuring all Americans.

Coverage through the Exchange will begin in every State on January 1, 2014, with enrollment beginning October 1, 2013. Recognizing that not all States may elect to establish a State-based Exchange by this statutory deadline, the Affordable Care Act directs the Secretary of HHS to establish and operate an FFE in any State that does not elect to do so, or will not have an operable Exchange for the 2014 coverage year, as determined by January 1, 2013.

As discussed in the Exchange final rule[1] and described more fully in this guidance, States will have the option to enter into a Partnership with an FFE. Under a State Partnership model, a State may administer plan management functions, in-person consumer assistance functions, or both. In non-Partnership FFE States, FFEs will perform these functions.

To the greatest extent possible, HHS intends to work with States to preserve the traditional responsibilities of State insurance departments when establishing an FFE. Additionally, HHS will seek to harmonize FFE policies with existing State programs and laws wherever possible.

In States where an FFE operates without a State Partnership, HHS will carry out all Exchange functions, including consulting with stakeholders and participating in formal consultation with Indian tribes; certifying, recertifying, and decertifying QHPs; determining individuals' eligibility for enrollment in a QHP through the Exchange and for insurance affordability programs; and supporting consumers, issuers, and other stakeholders through technical assistance and enrollment facilitation resources. HHS will administer these functions consistent with the Exchange final rule, which established minimum Federal standards for major Exchange business areas while leaving much flexibility and discretion to Exchanges to design processes and procedures that reflect local market dynamics.

This guidance describes the general approach regarding how HHS will interpret and implement this regulatory flexibility in operating an FFE. We focus on issues related to plan management, eligibility and enrollment of individuals, and key features of the Federally-facilitated Small Business Health Options Program (FF-SHOP).

We are committed to seeking ongoing input on FFE policy and operations from interested stakeholders, including States, issuers, and consumers.

HHS has articulated four "guiding principles" for FFEs, based on comments received on the Exchange establishment and eligibility proposed rules and other input from stakeholders:

1) *Commitment to consumers:* Our goal is to ensure that consumers in all 50 States and the District of Columbia have access to high-quality, affordable health coverage options through a State-based Exchange, Partnership Exchange, or FFE. We will continuously seek to improve policies and processes in each Exchange in pursuit of a positive and seamless consumer experience.
2) *Market parity:* HHS will work to harmonize market requirements inside and outside of an FFE to promote the competitiveness of each FFE, minimize administrative burden for issuers, and ensure consumer protections.
3) *Leveraging the traditional State role:* HHS recognizes the significant experience and the traditional role of States in many core areas of FFE operations. We will seek to capitalize on existing State policies, capabilities, and infrastructure that can also assist in implementing some of the components of an FFE.
4) *Engagement with States and other stakeholders:* HHS will seek input from a variety of stakeholders to support and inform decision-making. We will communicate our progress regularly so that affected parties understand how each FFE is developing and have adequate time to prepare for successful participation.

II. State Partnership in a Federally-Facilitated Exchange

As outlined in the preamble to the Exchange final rule, States will have the option to enter into a Partnership with an FFE to support administration and operation of selected functions. Specifically, a State Partner may assume primary responsibility for the plan management function, in-person consumer assistance functions (including oversight and management of Exchange Navigators), or both. These options are separate and distinct from the options available to States for conducting eligibility determinations as outlined in 45 CFR 155.302 and discussed in greater detail in the eligibility and enrollment portion of this guidance document.

To ensure operational efficiency, the State Partner in plan management will conduct all plan management activities. This includes conducting all analyses and reviews necessary to support QHP certification. In addition, the State Partner will collect and transmit necessary data to HHS in a specific format, and manage certified QHPs.

In a State Partnership in consumer assistance, the State Partner will administer, oversee, and support in-person application assistance and other in-person assistance to consumers, including a Navigator Program, to assist consumers in understanding, comparing, and enrolling in coverage, among other functions. Other in-person assistance may include supporting consumers in filing an application, obtaining an eligibility determination or reporting a change in status, comparing coverage options, and selecting and enrolling in a QHP. We note that HHS will be responsible for certain centralized functions, such as management of the Web site and consumer hotline, in States where a consumer assistance Partnership is operating.

The following chart provides additional detail on the specific functions that fall under the plan management and consumer assistance Partnership options.

States can choose to be responsible for the day-to-day management of the plan management and/or consumer assistance functions under these Partnership options; however, HHS, by law, retains authority over each FFE. Specifically, as HHS is responsible for Exchange implementation, we will approve State Partners to perform plan management or consumer assistance functions, and retain authority over inherently governmental functions (certification of specific QHPs, selection of Navigators, etc.) carried out by the State Partner on an ongoing basis. HHS will enter into agreements with State

Partners to establish and memorialize roles and responsibilities, and outline specific workflows, deliverables, review standards, and timeframes. State Partners may elect to use the Federal plan management system to carry out plan management activities.

Chart 1. Summary of State Partner Functions in Plan Management, Consumer Assistance

Partnership Model	Overview of State Functions

Plan Management	• Develop and implement processes and standards for QHP certification, recertification, and decertification within FFE parameters
	• Conduct QHP certification review including:
	  • Licensure and good standing
	  • Service area
	  • Network adequacy
	  • Essential community providers
	  • Marketing oversight
	  • Accreditation, on the timeline to be established in future rulemaking
	  • Essential health benefits standards
	  • Actuarial value standards, including variations for cost-sharing reductions, as well as cost-sharing limits
	  • Discriminatory benefit design
	  • Benefits for meaningful difference
	  • Rates (new and increases), including compliance with market rating reforms
	• Perform QHP issuer account management
	• Perform QHP oversight and monitoring, including marketing
	• Collect necessary data from issuers
	• Verify accreditation status and data if any accreditation data will be displayed on the Internet portal
	• Collect and display quality data (in future rulemaking)
	• Coordinate with HHS on quality rating and enrollee satisfaction survey (in future rulemaking)

Consumer Assistance	• Support, administer, and oversee Navigator program
	• Provide other in-person assistance to help consumers, including:
	  • Filing an application
	  • Receiving an eligibility determination
	  • Reporting changes during the coverage year
	  • Renewing coverage
	  • Comparing and selecting a coverage option
	  • Enrolling in a QHP

A State electing a State Partnership must designate the appropriate agency that has the authority and capacity to carry out the relevant functions. We encourage States considering a State Partnership to engage in technical assistance and consultation with HHS as soon as possible to ensure the successful operations of the Partnership. States may use grant funding available under section 1311 of the Affordable Care Act for the development, refinement, and testing of functions under a State Partnership model.

Consistent with the flexibility for States choosing to operate a State-based Exchange (including conditional approval and extensions of grant funding availability), HHS designed these Partnership options particularly to leverage traditional State roles, as well as help States that want to transition to a State-based Exchange. We strongly encourage States that are not considering a State-based Exchange to consider the Partnership options. The State Partnership model enables States and HHS to work together to operate an Exchange in an effective and seamless way for QHP issuers, consumers, small businesses, and others.[2]

III. Approach to Key Exchange Functions in a Federally-facilitated Exchange

The remainder of this guidance describes how an FFE will implement major business functions where there is no State Partnership.

The policy objectives of the FFE include, but are not limited to, offering a positive consumer experience, creating an attractive and viable market for issuers, working quickly and effectively with States, and reducing administrative and operational burdens on all Exchange participants. As HHS pursues these objectives, we are mindful of our ultimate responsibility to construct a functional, operationally sound Exchange that provides excellent service to customers. HHS also has a responsibility to develop safeguards and processes to protect and oversee public dollars spent for advance payments of the premium tax credit (APTC) and cost-sharing reductions (CSR).

HHS is developing a unified FFE administrative infrastructure supporting all FFEs that can address a wide range of State needs. As described at the end of this document, HHS will look to States, consumers, issuers, health care providers, employers, and other local stakeholders to provide input on the development of an FFE in each State where an FFE operates.

Plan Management in a Federally-facilitated Exchange

The plan management function includes all aspects of QHP certification, monitoring, oversight, and management. This guidance focuses primarily on the QHP certification process.[3]

QHP Certification Process

An FFE's role and authority are limited to the certification and management of participating QHPs, and do not extend beyond the Exchange or affect otherwise applicable State law governing which health insurance products may be sold in the individual and small group markets. Several QHP certification standards rely on reviews that State departments of insurance (DOI) do not currently conduct. Therefore, HHS will evaluate each potential QHP against all applicable certification standards, either by confirming the outcome of a State's review (as in the case of licensure) or by performing the review. FFEs will consider completed State work to support this evaluation where possible.

To ensure a robust QHP market in each State where an FFE operates, and to promote consumer choice among QHPs, at least in the first year HHS intends to certify as a QHP any health plan that meets all certification standards. In future years, HHS will analyze the QHP certification process and may identify improvements or changes to this process.

States will continue to perform their traditional regulatory role for issuers and health plans, and an issuer that wishes to offer QHPs through an FFE must meet both applicable State laws and requirements and QHP certification standards. Recognizing this, each FFE intends to complete all reviews and analyses in advance of the final QHP certification deadline to allow issuers to file with their respective State DOIs and seek any additional necessary approvals.

HHS intends to release the QHP Issuer Application in early 2013 through an electronic plan management system. HHS will also make the application available to the general public. The application will outline the data and other documents that we believe are necessary to illustrate compliance with QHP certification standards. In 2012, HHS will release for public comment a model application that includes relevant issuer, rate, and benefit data standards to help issuers prepare for the submission process. HHS also intends to release a rate and benefit data submission module shortly after the release of the QHP Issuer Application and will begin a plan-level review in early spring 2013. We anticipate that FFEs will complete agreements with issuers of certified

QHPs in late summer 2013, as described in the next section. Open enrollment for the 2014 coverage year will begin on October 1, 2013.

As indicated in the final rule on Reinsurance, Risk Corridors, and Risk Adjustment,[4] HHS will release both a draft and final notice of benefit and payment parameters with additional detail on key parameters for finalizing issuers' data submissions, including user fee, risk adjustment, risk corridor, and reinsurance methodologies.

Chart 2. High-level Overview of QHP Certification Process

QHP Certification Process	
Issuer-level Review (Vehicle: QHP Issuer Application)	
QHP Certification Standard	*High-level Summary of FFE Activity*
Licensure and good standing	Confirm State licensure and compliance with State solvency and other related requirements.
Network adequacy	In States meeting minimum Federal standards, verify State review. Otherwise, review network adequacy data submitted in QHP Issuer Application.
Essential community providers (ECPs)	Collect information on inclusion of ECPs in provider networks and review for sufficiency.
Accreditation	Confirm accreditation status, depending on certification year (as described in future rulemaking).
Program attestations	Ensure submission of required attestations (for example, attestation of compliance with marketing standards).
Plan-level Review (Vehicle: Rate and Benefit Data Submission) (Note: States continue to perform their traditional regulatory role)	
QHP Certification Standard	*High-level Summary of FFE Activity*
Essential health benefits	Confirm coverage of essential health benefits.
Actuarial value standards, including variations for cost-sharing reductions	Confirm actuarial value levels of potential QHPs, including compliance with standards related to cost-sharing reductions, cost-sharing limits, and variations to cost-sharing structures.
Discriminatory benefit design	Conduct plan-level analysis (such as outlier analysis) targeting areas where discrimination would most likely occur.
Meaningful difference	Conduct review for meaningful difference across QHPs offered by the same issuer to ensure that a manageable number of distinct plan options are offered.
Service area	Confirm that service area is at least one county or that smaller service area is necessary, nondiscriminatory, and in the interest of consumers.
Rates (new and increases)	Review new rates and rate increase justifications for reasonableness, including confirmation of compliance with market rating reforms.

Other Plan Management Functions

An FFE will also perform activities in addition to QHP certification, including QHP issuer account management, QHP oversight, and recertification. HHS plans to provide technical assistance and support to issuers on an ongoing basis following QHP certification through designated account managers.

The Account Manager will serve as the issuer's point of contact, coordinate technical assistance and communication across business areas, and assist issuers in navigating FFE and State requirements. HHS expects States (even those not participating in the plan management Partnership model) to play a primary role in areas of traditional State responsibility, with an FFE assuming a primary role in oversight in areas that fall outside the scope of States' regulatory authority; are Exchange-specific; or where Federal funds are involved. An FFE will coordinate its oversight and management activities with State regulators to streamline processes and reduce duplication of effort to the extent possible. In addition to ensuring ongoing compliance with QHP certification requirements, an FFE will also recertify QHPs periodically in future years. Other plan management functions that an FFE will perform include:

- *Reconsiderations of FFE certification decisions*: Each FFE will provide a process for issuers to request reconsiderations of QHP certification decisions.
- *QHP agreements*: HHS will enter into agreements with QHP issuers to memorialize certification and procedural requirements. This process will take place after the end of the QHP certification process.
- *Plan data display on the FFE Web site*: Each FFE will allow issuers to view and validate plan data before public display on the FFE Web site.
- *Recertification and the annual process for plan review*: An FFE will establish a process for recertification. At a minimum, each FFE will annually ensure compliance with issuer licensure, solvency, accreditation data, review network adequacy and plan-level rate and benefit data, and consider changes to service areas and changes in ownership, mergers, or acquisitions.
- *Decertification*: Each FFE will establish a process for decertification of QHPs that fall out of compliance with QHP certification standards.
- *User fees*: HHS will support the ongoing operations of FFEs by developing and implementing a system to calculate and collect user

fees from participating issuers. HHS will include detailed information about FFE user fees in the draft notice of payment and benefit parameters that we plan to release this fall.

Accreditation and Quality Reporting

The Affordable Care Act includes several provisions to improve the quality of care delivered by QHPs and increase the availability of quality data that can inform plan selection. Specifically, the Affordable Care Act requires QHP issuers to implement quality improvement strategies, enhance patient safety through certain contracting requirements, and publicly report quality data. In addition, the Affordable Care Act directs the Secretary to develop and administer a rating system and an enrollee satisfaction survey system, the results of which will be available to consumers. HHS intends to issue future rulemaking on quality reporting and disclosure requirements.

QHP issuers participating in an FFE will be required to be accredited by an accrediting entity and comply with quality reporting requirements that HHS will specify in future rulemaking. HHS intends to propose a phased approach to accreditation and quality data reporting and display in an FFE to accommodate new QHP issuers and Medicaid plans without Exchange or accreditation experience.

HHS also intends to propose a phased process for recognizing accrediting entities. In phase one, the entities that HHS believes will be equipped to provide the statutorily required accreditation review by 2013 certification – the National Committee for Quality Assurance (NCQA) and URAC – would be recognized as accrediting entities on an interim basis subject to conditions. In phase two, we would adopt an application and review process for the recognition of additional accrediting entities.

We intend to propose that an FFE will accept existing health plan accreditation from NCQA and URAC on issuers' commercial or Medicaid lines of business in the same state in which the issuer is seeking to offer Exchange coverage until the fourth year of certification (for example, 2016 certification for the 2017 coverage year). HHS intends to propose that QHP issuers without this existing accreditation must schedule this accreditation in their first year of certification and be accredited on QHP policies and procedures by the second year of certification. By the fourth year of certification, all QHP issuers must be accredited on the QHP product type having fulfilled the requirements to submit performance data to the accrediting entity.

Similarly, HHS intends to propose a phased approach to new quality reporting and display requirements for all Exchanges and expects that State-based Exchanges may adopt a similar approach prior to final regulatory standards. For example, HHS intends to propose that reporting requirements related to all QHP issuers will start in 2016. HHS intends to support the calculation of the QHP-specific quality rating for all QHP issuers in all Exchanges. The QHP-specific quality rating would be available for display in 2016 open enrollment for the 2017 coverage year. In the interim, an FFE will display existing Consumer Assessments of Healthcare Providers and Systems (CAHPS) results from accredited commercial and/or Medicaid product lines when these existing CAHPS data are available for the same QHP product types and adult/child populations (for example, HMO Adult CAHPS results for HMO QHPs, Child CAHPS results for child-only QHPs). FFEs will not display other data drawn from the accreditation data, such as clinical measures results.

HHS intends to engage in rulemaking for quality reporting and disclosure requirements for all Exchanges. HHS also intends to solicit stakeholder input on the most effective ways to align the quality reporting and display requirements for QHPs in 2016 and beyond with related quality measurement initiatives across HHS (for example, the National Quality Strategy, section 2717 of the Affordable Care Act, and quality reporting requirements under Medicare and Medicaid).

Eligibility for Insurance Affordability Programs and Enrollment in the Individual Market

Each FFE will determine individuals' eligibility for enrollment in a QHP and for APTC and CSR; assess or determine eligibility for Medicaid and the Children's Health Insurance Program (CHIP); and assist eligible individuals in comparing, selecting, and enrolling in a QHP. The Exchange final rule and the Medicaid and CHIP final rule[5] lay out a streamlined process for determining eligibility for enrollment in a QHP through the Exchange, APTC, CSR, Medicaid, and CHIP. Achieving this vision requires a high level of coordination across programs in information technology, program management, and business operations. In the FFE context, HHS is developing a dynamic Web-based system to support eligibility determinations for all insurance affordability programs, and an eligibility workforce to handle exceptions and manual processing of applications. We will continue to work with States to ensure coordination with State eligibility processes.

Determining Eligibility

Together, the creation of Exchanges, along with insurance reforms, APTC, CSR, and the changes to Medicaid eligibility established in the Affordable Care Act, will expand access to health benefits to millions of consumers.

To offer a seamless consumer experience, each FFE must allow consumers to receive eligibility determinations for multiple programs using a single, streamlined application, regardless of where consumers submit their applications. HHS is creating a model electronic application for potential use by all States, including States where an FFE operates. In addition to the Web- and paper-based eligibility applications, HHS will create model notices consistent with those established in the Exchange and Medicaid final rules. The application and notices will be written in plain language and will be tested to ensure that consumers understand the content and requirements. FFEs will also provide information to consumers in a manner that is accessible to people with disabilities and those with limited English proficiency.

A well-coordinated eligibility process is essential to the consumer experience and we believe that it can be accomplished through the eligibility determination process outlined below. Consistent with 45 CFR 155.302, there will be two approaches for determining applicants' eligibility for Medicaid and CHIP based on MAGI for applications submitted to an FFE:

(1) The FFE will determine Medicaid and CHIP eligibility based on MAGI and electronically transmit the determination and all information for any eligible applicants to the State Medicaid and CHIP agency. The Medicaid and CHIP agency will accept the FFE's determination and provide for enrollment in Medicaid or CHIP coverage.
(2) The FFE will conduct assessments of Medicaid and CHIP eligibility based on MAGI as part of the determination of eligibility for APTC and CSR. The FFE will electronically transmit all information for any potentially eligible applicants to the State Medicaid and CHIP agency, which will make final determinations and notify the Exchange if the State Medicaid or CHIP agency finds that the applicant is ineligible.

Under either option, an FFE will assess or determine Medicaid and CHIP eligibility based on the State's applicable Medicaid and CHIP MAGI-based income standards, citizenship and immigration status, other eligibility requirements, and standard verification rules and procedures consistent with 42 CFR parts 435 and 457. HHS will release more detailed information about the eligibility determination process in future guidance.[6]

Key Areas of Engagement: Information Technology

In the following areas, coordination across an FFE, Medicaid, and CHIP is particularly important. HHS is working with State Medicaid and CHIP agencies in these and other areas to reduce administrative burden and further streamline the process for consumers.

- *Verification of an existing eligibility determination for Medicaid or CHIP*: In order to determine eligibility for APTC and CSR, and to ensure that an FFE is able to direct individuals to the appropriate program, each FFE will connect with the State Medicaid and CHIP agencies to verify whether an individual has already been determined eligible for Medicaid or CHIP.
- *Verification of income*: Each FFE will use data from certain State-based data sources used by State Medicaid and CHIP agencies to support assessments or determinations of eligibility for Medicaid and CHIP and to support eligibility determinations for APTC and CSR. These data sources include the State Wage Information Collection Agency (SWICA) and the State unemployment benefits agency.
- *Electronic transmission and receipt of application information for eligible/potentially eligible individuals*: An FFE will electronically transmit application data and other information for individuals determined eligible or assessed as potentially eligible for Medicaid or CHIP to the State Medicaid and CHIP agencies in a timely and secure manner. All FFEs will also receive application data and other information electronically from the State Medicaid and CHIP agency for applicants screened as potentially eligible for enrollment in a QHP, APTC, or CSR.

Key Areas of Engagement: Business Processes and Customer Services

- *Identifying eligibility model and rules for Medicaid and CHIP*: Each FFE and the respective State Medicaid and CHIP agencies will work together to identify roles and responsibilities related to Medicaid and CHIP eligibility determinations. Whether the FFE is determining eligibility or conducting an assessment of eligibility for Medicaid and CHIP, the FFE will obtain relevant information from the State, such as regarding the State's applicable MAGI-based income standards for Medicaid and CHIP.

- *Customer service to support eligibility and enrollment*: All FFEs will have a call center for individuals. The FFE, the State Medicaid and CHIP agencies, and other entities providing customer service in a State, including the Department of Insurance, will coordinate closely to share information, create protocols to help consumers resolve issues, and ensure smooth handoffs among entities.
- *Outreach and education*: The FFE's outreach and education efforts will be most effective when coordinated closely with the relevant State agencies and stakeholders. This coordination could include ensuring that messaging is synchronized to the greatest extent possible.
- *Notices*: There are a number of potential interactions between the consumers, FFEs, and State Medicaid and CHIP agencies. To ensure that consumers receive clear, accurate, and actionable information about their eligibility for enrollment in a QHP and for insurance affordability programs, an FFE and the State Medicaid and CHIP agencies will work closely to ensure that notices to applicants clearly describe next steps and customer service contact information. We intend to provide further detail on notices.
- *Program planning and management*: Some families will have members with coverage in Medicaid or CHIP and FFEs; in addition, individuals may transition between programs as circumstances change. To offer the best possible support for these individuals and families, an FFE and the State Medicaid and CHIP agencies will work together to identify and resolve issues that cross programs.
- *Appeals*: We are evaluating how the Exchange appeals process will coordinate with State Medicaid and CHIP agencies, and we intend to provide further guidance and proposed rulemaking on this topic in the future.

Process for Engagement

HHS and State Medicaid and CHIP agencies will develop project plans and formal and informal processes to support eligibility determinations, inform the development of and updates to standard operating procedures and enrollment processes, to create a positive and seamless consumer experience. Both the Exchange and the Medicaid and CHIP eligibility rules outline mutual responsibilities and call for a memorandum of understanding to specifically identify roles, responsibilities, and timelines. Data sharing agreements and standards for information exchanges will be particularly critical. Further guidance and toolsets will be forthcoming to delineate tasks, schedules, and specifications for development and testing of FFE and Medicaid and CHIP interactions. HHS plans to support the coordination effort with a cross-functional team covering eligibility operations; data sharing from the business, technology, and legal perspectives; and customer service, outreach, and education. HHS will continue to reach out to States to begin these discussions, and encourages State Medicaid and CHIP agencies to initiate dialogue.

Consumer Support, Outreach, and Education

HHS will conduct an outreach and education campaign to raise awareness of and promote enrollment in QHPs and insurance affordability programs through an FFE. As described earlier in this document, we encourage States to consider a State Partnership in consumer assistance. States already have relationships with local community and business organizations that will be critical for effective outreach and assistance to consumers.

FFEs will assist consumers in receiving eligibility determinations for all insurance eligibility programs, comparing and selecting QHPs, and enrolling in a QHP. FFEs will offer a Web site, toll-free hotline, and other in-person assistance, which will also be accessible to persons with disabilities and those with limited English proficiency.

FFEs will establish Navigator programs by awarding grants to eligible entities that can assist consumers in understanding insurance affordability programs, comparing and selecting QHPs, and interacting with QHP issuers, State agencies, and the FFE. Navigators will also conduct public education and outreach about Exchanges and provide referrals to other resources, as appropriate.

It is HHS' intent to award Navigator grants prior to 2014,[7] with the goal of establishing a fully operational Navigator program in every FFE by October 1, 2013, so that all entities and individuals serving as Navigators are fully trained, certified, and ready to serve consumers, including those with disabilities and limited English proficiency. In addition to the Navigator program, HHS envisions that consumers will be able to receive in-person assistance from a variety of other consumer resources, including agents and brokers.

HHS expects that licensed agents and brokers will continue to assist consumers in accessing health insurance, and will work with agents and brokers to promote enrollment through the Exchange.

To the extent permitted by a State, an FFE will permit agents and brokers to enroll individuals in a QHP "through an Exchange" if the agent or broker ensures that an individual completes the eligibility verification and enrollment application using the Exchange Internet site or the agent or broker's site that meets certain conditions; the Exchange transmits the enrollment information to the QHP issuer; and the agent or broker meets other applicable requirements (an agreement, training, and registration).

HHS will provide licensed agents and brokers with a portal to the FFE Web site if applicable standards are met.[8] The portal will allow agents and brokers to help individuals apply for eligibility for enrollment in a QHP and for insurance affordability programs, and if applicable, select and enroll in a QHP through an FFE.

To the extent permitted by a State, HHS intends to work with Web-based brokers that meet all applicable requirements to help consumers select health plans online.

Additionally, consistent with the Exchange final rule, HHS intends to use an application programming interface (API) to allow individuals to enroll in QHPs through an FFE with the assistance of Web brokers.

Other FFE Functions Related to Eligibility for Insurance Affordability Programs and Enrollment in the Individual Market

- *Management of QHP eligibility and enrollment data*: Each FFE will transmit eligibility and enrollment data to QHP issuers promptly, securely, and without undue delay, and will require issuers to acknowledge receipt of such information. Each FFE will reconcile eligibility and enrollment data. In addition, each FFE will need detailed, up-to-date information on premium payments and coverage effective dates from QHP issuers to administer APTC and CSR.
- *Establishment and maintenance of the Internet Web site*: HHS will establish and maintain an FFE Internet Web site. The Web site will provide a calculator that facilitates the comparison of out of pocket costs for available QHPs after the application of any APTC and CSR.

Federally Facilitated-SHOP

FF-SHOPs will provide small employers with new ways to offer employee health coverage, better information about coverage options, and easier benefit administration. In addition, small employers who participate in a SHOP may qualify for the small business health insurance premium tax credit of up to 50 percent of the employer contribution.

The Affordable Care Act defines the small group market as employers with 1-100 employees, but permits States to establish an upper limit of 50 employees in 2014 and 2015. For purposes of FF-SHOP eligibility, HHS will adopt State definitions of the small group market in 2014 and 2015. HHS will count full-time equivalent employees to determine employer size consistent with the definitions in the Public Health Service Act as required by the law.

FF-SHOPs will provide a number of tools and resources to assist employers, employees, and agents and brokers in evaluating coverage options available through the FF-SHOP and selecting a health plan. For example, the FF-SHOP Web site will allow employers to model various choice scenarios (such as by changing the employer contribution percentage) before making a final selection. The FF-SHOP will also support employers and small group issuers by collecting a single, aggregated payment from each employer and distributing that payment to QHP issuers based on participating employees' plan selections. Other functions that an FF-SHOP will offer include:

- *Health plan data collection*: An FF-SHOP will accept changes in rates quarterly, with new rates applying for an entire coverage year beginning at the time of initial plan issuance or annual renewal.
- *Multi-State employers*: Multi-State employers participating in the FF-SHOP will offer coverage to all eligible employees either through the FF-SHOP serving the employer's primary place of business or through the State-based or FF-SHOP serving each employee's primary worksite.
- *Administrative support*: An FF-SHOP will provide for premium aggregation and other office functions, such as employer billing, receipt of payments, disbursements to plans, and payment reconciliation.
- *Consumer services*: FF-SHOPs will provide consumer support, including informational resources and application support through an Internet Web site, call center, and outreach and education.

- *Role of agents and brokers*: HHS anticipates that agents, brokers, and other producers will be a primary channel small businesses use to access coverage through an FF-SHOP. In addition to providing assistance with enrollment activities, HHS anticipates that agents and brokers will continue to be a primary point of contact for a variety of administrative, billings, and claims-related issues, and will work with FF-SHOPs to assist their clients in resolving these issues.

HHS will release future guidance on a number of topics related to the development and operation of FF-SHOPs, including policy issues related to States' small group markets, employer contribution models, and specific operational decisions, such as payment grace periods and maximum allowable new hire waiting periods.

IV. Stakeholder Input

HHS will work closely with local stakeholders to implement each FFE, including in States where a Partnership is operating. HHS is committed to creating a transparent process for FFE development in each State, and will seek input from stakeholders and provide technical assistance to those stakeholders working with an FFE. We anticipate that HHS will continue to engage with the stakeholder community through forums and workshops to implementation and operational issues and outreach and enrollment strategies. HHS will convene implementation sessions and other venues for discussion and input on FFE operations. HHS is also exploring with the National Association of Insurance Commissioners (NAIC) whether an advisory board can or should be created in States where such boards do not already exist. We welcome input on opportunities for HHS to work with local stakeholders including consumers, plans, providers and employers, to develop a successful Exchange in every State.

HHS also anticipates stakeholder consultation focused on FF-SHOPs. HHS recognizes that the successful operation of an FF-SHOP will benefit from the wealth of experience in State agencies. HHS intends to work with States to engage stakeholders and gather input, and believes that drawing on State expertise, discussing issues of joint interest, and exploring actions to facilitate the development of employee choice models of small group insurance will benefit the employer and employee experience in FF-SHOPs.

HHS recognizes the potential that FFEs will have to improve access to health coverage for American Indians and Alaska Natives in States that do not establish State-based Exchanges. Accordingly, we intend to consult with Tribes both in the development of FFEs and on an ongoing basis, consistent with the Presidential memorandum of November 5, 2009 and HHS' tribal consultation policy. The Affordable Care Act and the Exchange final rule include a number of provisions that uniquely affect American Indians and Alaska Natives, including but not limited to special enrollment periods and cost-sharing reductions for eligible individuals or individuals who obtain covered services from an Indian Health Provider. In addition, the Exchange final rule states that section 206 of the Indian Health Care Improvement Act, related to payment of Indian health providers by third party payers, will apply to QHPs participating in an Exchange. HHS intends to consult with Tribes to implement FFE policies that impact American Indians and Alaska Natives, and will release more specific information about this consultation and policies unique to these populations in the near future.

Educating Exchange stakeholders about FFE policy and providing technical assistance to States, issuers, consumer advocates, and the general public will be a key goal of HHS' outreach effort. Stakeholder input will both inform the implementation of policies articulated in this guidance, and future decision-making. The perspectives and feedback of local stakeholders will be particularly critical as each FFE begins to review and certify QHPs, offer plan selections to potential enrollees, conduct eligibility determinations, and enroll individuals into coverage.

Finally, we note that additional information on the operation of Exchanges in the U.S. Territories will be included in a future guidance.[9]

End Notes

[1] The final rule was published at 77 Fed. Reg. 18310 (March 27, 2012) (to be codified at 45 C.F.R. parts 155, 156 and 157).

[2] In light of public comments received on the final Medicaid and Exchange eligibility regulations, we intend to propose a regulation for further comment to consider amending the final rules regarding Medicaid eligibility determinations made by Exchanges. In particular we will seek further comment regarding ways States can ensure a coordinated system when engaging non-profits and private contractors in the process of making Medicaid eligibility evaluations, while having government agencies make eligibility determinations. We believe this potential change is consistent with current State practices and plans and will seek input in the rule making process.

[3] We note that, for references throughout this section to "health plans," "qualified health plans," health insurance issuers" and "qualified health plan issuers," the definitions of these

respective terms established in the Exchange final rule apply. 77 Fed. Reg., at 18445 (to be codified at 45 CFR 155.20). We recognize that States frequently collect health plan information at the "product" level, and we intend to include a definition of product in forthcoming guidance to ensure clear communications between the FFE and State DOIs on this topic.

[4] Published at 77 Fed. Reg. 17220 (March 23, 2012).

[5] Published at 77 Fed. Reg. 17144 (Mar. 23, 2012).

[6] As specified in the Medicaid and CHIP final rules, State Medicaid and CHIP agencies will accept applications and make Medicaid and CHIP eligibility determinations. The FFE will also make Medicaid and CHIP eligibility assessments and/or determinations for individuals who apply directly to the FFE. Within this context, the Federal government will not charge States for eligibility assessments or determinations for Medicaid and CHIP based on applications submitted to the FFE.

[7] This and some other activities are subject to the availability of Federal funds.

[8] *See* 77 Fed. Reg. at 18449 (to be codified at 45 C.F.R. §155.220).

[9] The term "State" means the 50 States and the District of Columbia. Therefore, there will be no federally-facilitated Exchange in a territory that does not choose to establish a State-based Exchange.

INDEX